Trusting God in Times and Seasons of Change

Trusting God in Times and Seasons of Change

by

Dr. Valerie S. DePastino

Christian Publishing Services, Inc.
Tulsa, Oklahoma

Unless otherwise indicated, all Scripture quotations are taken from the *King James Version* of the Bible.

Some quotations are from *The Amplified Bible, New Testament* (AMP). Copyright © 1954, 1958 by The Lockman Foundation, La Habra, California, and *The Amplified Bible, Old Testament* (AMP). Copyright © 1962, 1964 by Zondervan Publishing House, Grand Rapids, Michigan.

Trusting God in Times and Seasons of Change
ISBN 0-88144-138-4

P. O. Box 31
Southington, Connecticut 06489

Published by Christian Publishing Services, Inc.
P. O. Box 55388
Tulsa, Oklahoma 74155

Printed in the United States of America.

Dedication

They that trust in the Lord shall be as mount Zion....

Psalm 124:1

To everything there is a season and a time....

Ecclesiastes 3:1

...are changed into the same image from glory to glory.

2 Corinthians 3:18

I dedicate this book to the beautiful, ever growing, ever loving, brothers and sisters of Whole Life Ministries, Augusta, Georgia, and Sandra Kennedy, their pastor.

This family of believers has demonstrated a desire, and taken the effort to do whatever might be required, to be on the cutting edge of what God is doing. When Almighty God spoke to Sandra Kennedy about beginning Whole Life Ministries, He said, "Don't ask them where they have come from but where they are going."

Thanks for showing us all a willingness to change.

About the Cover

The cover of this book is very significant and has a spiritual message which complements the text. The portrait was painted under the inspiration of the Holy Spirit by a dear sister in Christ, Mary Jane Cross, and is entitled "Portrait in Time."

In order to fully understand the message of the painting, one must first see that the viewer is looking at the painting of God's clock from slightly above the level of the clock which is the side from which God views it. This a contrary to a straight-on view, which would be that of a "fence sitter," or of a view looking up from below, which would be from the perspective of an unsaved person. As Valerie's ministry is primarily to the Body of Christ, her books and teachings speak to the Church and are dedicated to helping the Body grow in maturity. Therefore, the message of the book is from the perspective of the believer.

The lower clock is a slightly distorted reflection of God's true clock. This is how the non-Christian people of the world view the things of God. The world can only see a reflection of what God really intended for us. (First Corinthians 13:12 describes this situation very well when it says, **For now we see through a glass darkly ....)** The people of the world think they are seeing the real thing. However, what they see is a poor, distorted, and not-quite-distinct reflection of reality.

God's world of the spirit is the real world. God's clock and sense of time and the world's clock and sense of time are not the same.

Jesus, because He was God *and* man, was the first human with the ability to understand eternity. During His brief time of ministry, Jesus often made statements concerning His eternal being which could not be comprehended by natural men. After His death, resurrection, and ascension, Jesus said, in Revelation 1:18, that He was alive forevermore and that He had the keys of death and of hell. This was a fulfillment of what Jesus meant in John 10:10, when He said that He "had come to give abundant life."

Death robs people of time! Time is highly valued by mankind. However, it is as if the world is being held hostage by the very same time that it can never get enough of. Psalm 90:4 and Second Peter 3:8 teach us that **with the Lord one day is as a thousand years, and a thousand years as one day.** Jesus triumphed over death and time.

God's time holds endless promise! The clock of God is constantly running toward the conclusion of what we know as this world. When God's time for earth, and the time designated for us, runs out, this world will end in His eternal triumph over time.

The world's clock is winding down, also. However, it will end in defeat. Oh, there still will be eternity afterwards, but it will hold eternal death — separation from God — for those who do not know Him personally.

Only as long as Time continues to run will men and women be able to freely choose their destinies. When time is finished, all choices will already have been made by default, if not by decision. In Luke 11:23, Jesus declared that anyone who is not for Him is against Him. When time ends with that last trumpet, everyone's choice is sealed for *life* or *death* for all eternity. In Ephesians 5:16, we are warned to make the very most of time, for the days grow evil.

We see that the hand of God is directly in control of His clock. In the reflection, there *is* no hand of God, because those in the world cannot or will not see the hand of God in their daily lives.

As Christians, we perceive God's hand in our lives and in the lives of those in the world. However, God is so big, and we are so small — according to our finite minds — that we often are unable to see beyond the footprints. The Holy Spirit, if we will let Him, will enable us to open our spiritual eyes.

When God reached down to earth into time, He came from the realm of the spirit and became flesh to accommodate us in our humanity. In Jesus, who had a body of flesh, we could be able to relate to the Father.

The colors used in "Portrait of Time" also are meaningful. Although thoughts of the passing of time and being in the endtime can be somewhat disturbing, they also are rich in eloquent anticipation of God's workings. Therefore, the colors used in this painting had to be rich and brilliant.

CONTENTS

1
The End Is Better Than the Beginning

God does not do something major in the earth without letting His people know first. In other words, He does not "spring something" on His Church. However, God's warnings and intimations of what He is going to do can only be heard by those with "hearing ears," those who are spiritually in tune with His Holy Spirit. Isaiah 42:9 is one of the *sure* promises of God.

> **Behold,** (That means "Look! Perceive what is happening!) **the former things are come to pass, and new things do I declare: before they spring forth I tell you of them.**

To those in this hour with listening ears to the Spirit, it should come as no surprise that we are in a season and a time of change. I believe that *right now* we are in one of the most critical times in God's plan for this earth.

The Spirit of God in June 1987 said that the years of 1988, 1989, and a flow over into 1990 would be a most critical time for the Body of Christ, in particular for the East Coast of the United States. He said it would be God's timing for the northern portions of this country. The working demonstration of the power of the Holy Spirit would come into operation in those areas during this period of time.

The purpose is for the Body in those regions to come in alignment with God's timing.

God is never behind time. His visions, plans, and purposes are never late. They are always exactly when God has set for them to happen.

A new season is coming upon the Body of Christ. We have heard about it through the past several years, but the timing is so close now that *we must listen* to what the Spirit is saying. God is going to have His way. He always wins. He always completes His plans and purposes *but not necessarily through the Church.* Our part is to get in alignment with what He is doing.

There is something He is bringing about for the northeastern United States, particularly the East Coast, to begin in 1990, and it is up to Christians in that area to get in position before God's move begins. In Isaiah 43: 18, 19, again we have a promise that I believe is as prophetic for our day as it was for Isaiah's day or for the days when Jesus came to earth the first time.

> **Remember ye not the former things, neither consider the things of old.**
>
> **Behold, I will do a new thing; now it shall spring forth; shall ye not know it? I will even make a way in the wilderness, and rivers in the desert.**

If God has a *sure* word for His Church — and He does — then we need to hear what He is saying. Look at Ezekiel 47:3-5 for a different perspective.

> **And when the man that had the line in his hand went forth eastward, he measured a**

> **thousand cubits, and he brought me through the waters; the waters were *to the ankles.*** (The correct translation is "to the sole of the foot."[1])
>
> **Again he measured a thousand, and brought me through the waters; the waters were to the knees. Again he measured a thousand, and brought me through; the waters were to the loins.**
>
> **Afterward he measured a thousand, and it was a river that I could not pass over: for the waters were risen, waters to swim in, a river that could not be passed over.**

In these verses, I believe the Holy Spirit showed me another dimension that is so important for today. To us, those verses can be applied spiritually this way:

When one is born again, one enters into the flow of the river, the flow of the Spirit of God. Water is a type and shadow of the Holy Spirit. But one enters into a very shallow dimension of the Spirit. When you first walk into a stream, river, or ocean, unless you jump in, you only touch it with the bottom of your foot. You are in the flow, but not in the full measure of that flow.

Then there are those who trust God and move out into the running water up to their knees. Others go a step farther and move out up to the waist. Up to that point, you have control over the water. However, once you move out into the current over your head, the water has authority over you. It is the same with the Spirit of God. If we want His fullness in our lives and His absolute authority, we must *jump in over our heads.*

---

[1] R. Laird Harris, Gleason L. Archer, Jr., Bruce K. Waltke. *Theological Word Book of the Old Testament* (Chicago: Moody Press, 1980), p. 65.

Now look at Ecclesiastes 7:8:

> **Better is the end of a thing than the beginning thereof: and the patient in spirit is better than the proud in spirit.**

That is a word of encouragement for the Church today and for individual Christians. Perhaps you have been walking with Christ for twenty years or longer, or maybe for just one month. It does not matter how long you have been in the walk of faith, the Word of God says *the end is going to be better.* As great as the excitement was when you were saved, when you came to the knowledge that God loved you, the end of your walk will be better.

Patience Is the Key

The key portion of Ecclesiastes 7:8 is **the patient in spirit** is better than the proud in spirit. Patience has never been my favorite word! I would like everything done yesterday. The Word says, however, that we need to be *patient* not to miss the timing of God and not to miss the move or the flow of His plan. *Proud in spirit* means those who try to do something on their own.

Some say, "I can do it. I do not need to wait for God's timing."

No, the Word says that the end is better than the beginning for those who are *patient,* not for those who are *proud in spirit.*

Habbakkuk 3:2 says:

> **O Lord, I have heard thy speech, and was afraid: O Lord, revive thy work in the midst of the years, in the midst of the years make known; in wrath remember mercy.**

Many of us could pray that same prayer to Almighty God, except that many have heard the word of the Holy Spirit about a coming new wave and are not afraid, but almost apathetic. Many Christians have lost their zeal. Many have lost the stirring in their spirits. Many are still just touching the water, and many others are knee deep or waist deep, but few are being totally carried by the current of the Holy Spirit. Not very many Christians have jumped in and let the Spirit of God totally carry them.

We do not know how long it will be before Jesus comes. It could be another twenty years, or another one hundred years, or longer. If there is a cry that *should* be coming out of the Church, it is, **O, Lord, revive thy work in the midst of the years.** We do not know how many years we have, but we should be praying for the Holy Spirit to once again stir His people.

When you became born again, you started to run a race. The Apostle Paul uses imagery from athletics often in his letters, because his time was the heyday of Greek sports. The athletic part of the culture of Greece permeated the entire Roman empire. Much like today, people thronged to watch the Olympic and other races, wrestling, and discus throwing, among other sports. Paul knew everyone to whom he wrote could relate to the word pictures likening the spiritual walk to races.

In Philippians 3:13,14 (AMP), Paul wrote about spiritual progress and holy ambition in terms of a race.

> **I do not consider, brethren, that I have captured and made it my own [yet]; but one thing I**

> **do — it is my one aspiration: forgetting what lies behind and straining forward to what lies ahead,**
>
> **I press on toward the goal to win the [supreme and heavenly] prize to which God in Christ Jesus is calling us upward.**

God is not calling us to the right, nor to the left. He is not calling us backward. There is an upward, or *onward,* goal. Paul was saying that you are to forget the past when you become born again and a new creation. You are to focus all your thoughts on moving forward in Him. There should be a constant progression, a constant ascension into the things of God, a pressing in to the very being of God.

Pressing on **to the prize of the mark of the high calling** (KJV) is calling us upward in Christ. Every race that has a beginning has an ending, does it not? There is the prize at the end of the race to look forward to. Another book that talks about races is Hebrews:

> **Wherefore seeing when we also are compassed about with so great a cloud of witnesses, let us lay aside every weight, and the sin which doth so easily beset us, and let us *run with patience* the race that is set before us.**
>
> **Hebrews 12:1**

There is that word *patience* again! Winning a race requires patience. Let us say that we are at the starting point of a race, the place each of us has been at one time or another. Before each of us when we were born again was a path, or a race, that has been set for us. And the writer of Hebrews is saying that a "great cloud of witnesses" is watching the race around us. They are cheering us on toward the goal God has set for us.

Lay Aside the Weights

I cannot run your race, and you cannot run mine. I cannot win your prize, and you cannot win mine. Each has to run his own race.

The writer of Hebrews goes on to say that we must lay aside every weight that holds us back, that keeps us from running at our best speed. At one time in my life, I taught physical education and coached for races. One of the key things in training for marathons was to fasten weights around the ankles of the runners and have them practice wearing the weights. Then on the day of the race, the weights were left off. There is a certain amount of agility and speed possible to someone who has practiced with weights that is not there for someone who has not.

The writer of Hebrews is saying we have already begun our races, and now is the time to lay aside the weights. Lay aside sin in your life which so easily besets you and is going to slow you down. Keeping the weights does not necessarily mean that you will not run your race, but it means you will be slower than necessary. You might not reach certain points along your path during the right season of God. It might be an acceptable race, but not a perfect one.

Church, we can no longer settle for that which is good or acceptable. We must do God's perfect will to be part of the endtime army. The anointing that carried us in time past will not be the same anointing for this move of the Spirit of God.[2] That anointing

---

[2] DePastino, Dr. Valerie S. *Endime Commissions Endtime Anointings Ezra 8:36* (Tulsa: Christian Publishing Services, Inc. Copyright © 1988 by Dr. Valerie S. DePastino).

was perfect for that season, but not for the one God is bringing forth today.

Today, we must lay aside the weights and press forward in the race to make sure that we are in the right position and in the right timing of God as never before.

Ecclesiastes 3:11 says that God has made everything beautiful in His time. That verse in *The Amplified Bible* also says that eternity has been planted in our hearts in such a way that no man can find out what God has done from beginning to end. So we are to lay aside the weights and await God's time to make everything beautiful.

> **He has made everything beautiful in its time; He also has planted eternity in men's heart and mind [a divinely implanted sense of a purpose working through the ages which nothing under the sun, but only God, can satisfy], yet so that man cannot find out what God has done from the beginning to the end.**

The minute you accepted Jesus as your personal Lord and Savior, you were placed in this race. Forget the things that lie behind you. Lay aside the weights and cares of everyday life. Put aside the sins that remain in your life from the past. Press on, knowing that Jesus is running the race with you. Do not look to the right or to the left. Do not be distracted by the ways of the world. **Man cannot find out what God has done.**

Hebrews 12:2 says Jesus is not only the *author,* the one who "creates" the race, but the finisher of it. He is the very source of our faith. He is in every single step whether you are in the water to your ankles, your knees, your waist, or over your head.

If you have ever watched a marathon, you know that each runner has someone on the sideline at a certain point who hands him water, throws him a wet towel, or gives him an orange, potassium, or vitamins. This person is the source of the runner's help for the race. For the Christian, that "Person" is Jesus. He is our Source. However, if you look to the right or to the left, you will be distracted and miss seeing the help when He offers it.

2

Learn To Recognize God's Timing

If we want to run our race rightly, if we want to see the move of God, we must come into the timing of God individually and collectively. We must learn to recognize the timing of God and learn to walk in it, not in our own timing.

In Genesis 18, the story of the intercession of Abraham on behalf of Sodom and Gomorrah is found. God told Abraham that He was going to destroy those two towns. Abraham then began to intercede. He asked God to spare the towns if a certain number of righteous people could be found in them. Each time Abraham named a number, God agreed! But each time God could not find that many who were righteous. Finally Abraham went before God one more time and asked Him to spare the towns for the sake of only ten — and God agreed. However, ten righteous could not be found.

Abraham did not specifically ask God for the lives of his relatives to be spared. Apparently, he thought interceding for ten righteous would cover them. However, on account of Abraham's intercession and because of his own righteousness, God spared the lives of his nephew Lot and his family — except for Lot's wife, who disobeyed the angels, looked back at the destruction, and also was destroyed. Most Christians are familiar with that story. What most do not realize is that for us a comparable Scripture is Acts 16:31. If you believe on the Lord Jesus Christ, you will be saved *and all those of your household.*

Now when the angel of the Lord came to Lot and said, "I want you to take your sons-in-law, your daughters, and your wife, and go to the mountains," this family was being offered a place of safety. The "sons-in-law" were betrothed to the daughters but apparently the marriages had not yet been consummated, because the daughters are referred to as "virgins." In those days, a betrothal was almost as binding as the marriage. An engaged couple was considered as good as married. However, these two men elected not to accompany Lot and his family out of town. They probably thought he was crazy.

Sodom and Gomorrah, we understand from other references, were destroyed mainly because of sexual perversion. The Lord said the outcry of their sin was so grievous that He would **go down and see whether they have done altogether according to the cry of it, which is come unto me; and if not, I will know** (Gen. 18:21). More than likely, then, the "sons-in-law" were participants to some extent in that lifestyle, which is why they chose to stay.

At this point, God set a beginning line for Lot and his family. He also told them there would be a "finish line" — mountains some distance away where they would be safe. The angels told them to go quickly because they could not destroy Sodom and Gomorrah *until Lot and his family were safe.*

Lot told the angels he did not think they could get as far as the mountains and asked instead to be allowed to escape into a small city called Zoar (which means "little"). The angels agreed to spare that city for the sake of Lot, but insisted that he go quickly.

They said, "We cannot do what God has said until you are protected, Lot. Until you and your family are safe, we cannot move." (Gen. 19:22.)

Do Not Draw Back

Lot had to know the timing of God. When God says to move quickly, we had better know it is time to move! Perhaps Lot and his family were up to the waist in the water of God, so to speak, and just ready to jump in over their heads — when Lot's wife turned around. In God's timing, that was no time to look back. We are to forget those things which are behind when God moves us onward to somewhere else.

Lot's wife turned around and became a pillar of salt. Was God's promise that the end would be better than the beginning fulfilled in her case? No. That promise was made invalid by her choosing to look back.

Hebrews 10:38 says the **just shall live by faith.** *Just* is the same word in the Greek that is translated *righteous* in other places. But what comes immediately after those words in the same verse? The Holy Spirit added a condition: **but if any man draw back, my soul shall have no pleasure in him.** The end was not better for Lot's wife *because she drew back.*

In Acts 1:16,17, we see a person in Jesus' time who looked back and missed the promise.

> **Men and brethren, this scripture must needs have been fulfilled, which the Holy Ghost by the mouth of David spake before concerning Judas, which was guide to them that took Jesus.**
>
> **For he was numbered with us, and had obtained part of this ministry.**

Judas walked with Jesus as one of the original twelve disciples. He talked with Jesus, ate with Him, and saw the miracles. He was there when blind eyes were opened, when the deaf were made to hear, and when the lame walked. He was there when the loaves and fishes were multiplied. He was there when Lazarus was raised from the dead.

In Acts 1:20, Luke records that Peter went on to say:

> **For it is written in the book of Psalms, Let his habitation be desolate, and let no man dwell therein: and his bishopric let another take.**

Let his place be empty. No one can fill *your* place. If God has called you to do something — and God has called every single person in the Body of Christ to run a certain race — then no one else can do your work for you. Someone else may be given your place and earn the prize that should have been yours, but no one else can *really* do the things that were assigned to you. That person may have your place, but he will have his own things to do, his own race to run.

In Judas, we have another example of someone that began right. But was the end better than the beginning? No, it was not. Judas drew back and allowed Satan to enter and take possession of him.

That We Might Do the Works of God

In John 6:28, the apostle records that some people asked Jesus, **What shall we do, that we might work the works of God?** In the group of people listening to Jesus that day in Capernaum probably were Pharisees and Sadducees, as well as common people of the area. A mixture of people followed Him immediately after the miracles of multiplying the loaves and fishes. Now these people wanted to know how to open blind eyes, raise the dead, and multiply food.

Today, we also are saying, "Lord, how can we work Your works?"

We have heard of demonstrations of the power of God in the past, but we want to see them today for ourselves. The Church is going through a shaking and a transition period and needs to know how to do the works of God. We need to experience His power, not just know it exists as a positional truth. Look at how Jesus answered that question.

> **Jesus answered and said unto them, This is the work of God, that ye believe on him whom he hath sent.**
>
> **John 6:29**

In spite of the signs they had seen, they asked for a "sign."

> **They said therefore unto him, What sign showest thou then, that we may see, and believe thee? what dost thou work?**
>
> **John 6:30**

Another time, the Pharisees and Sadducees asked Him for a sign from heaven to "tempt" Him.

> **He answered and said unto them, When it is evening, ye say, it will be fair weather: for the sky is red.**
>
> **And in the morning, It will be foul weather today: for the sky is red and lowering. O ye hypocrites, ye can discern the face of the sky; but can ye not discern the signs of the times?**
>
> **A wicked and adulterous generation seeketh after a sign; and there shall no sign be given unto it, but the sign of the prophet Jonas. And he left them, and departed.**
>
> **Matthew 16:2-4**

He was saying to them, "You think you are so smart because you know weather signs. You can look at the sky and see what tomorrow will bring, but you do not know the ways of God!"

It was not just the Pharisees and Sadducees. Many of his followers wanted to have a spectacular sign from God. Remember? They had walked with Jesus, talked and ate with Jesus, and observed the miracles. They had heard His teachings. *Now* they still wanted "a sign!"

They pointed out that their ancestors had eaten manna in the desert and reminded Jesus of a saying based on that time: **He** (Moses) **gave them bread from heaven to eat** (v. 31).

> **Then Jesus said unto them, Verily, verily, I say unto you, Moses gave you not that bread from heaven; but my Father giveth you the true bread from heaven.**
>
> **For the bread of God is he which cometh down from heaven, and giveth life unto the world.**
>
> **Then said they unto him, Lord, evermore give us this bread.**

> **And Jesus said unto them, I am the bread of life: he that cometh to me shall never hunger; and he that believeth on me shall never thirst.**
>
> **John 6:32-35**

They were saying, "Lord, that sounds pretty good. All I have to do is eat a piece of bread to get the works? Don't butter it. Don't toast it. Just give it to me."

How many people in the Body of Christ want to work the works of God, but when God speaks to them and says, "You have to change, you have to move to this position, you have to step into a deeper measure of the flow of God," they do not want to do it.

We have heard the Lord say to lay aside the weights and get rid of the sin, yet we do not do it. God said not to look back, not to draw back, yet we do it. We have zeal. We have this excitement, this exuberance — yet we do not want to do what God says in order to get the works of God.

Jesus said, **I am the bread of life.** That should not be a surprising passage. Jesus said it many times concerning coming unto Him.

> **In the last day, that great day of the feast, Jesus stood and cried, saying, If any man thirst, let him come unto me, and drink.**
>
> **He that believeth on me, as the scripture hath said, out of his belly shall flow rivers of living water.**
>
> **John 7:37,38**

We often quote verse 38, but forget about verse 37. Rivers of living water are going to flow out of the bellies of *those who come unto Jesus and drink.* Jesus offers bread and water. Those who come to Him are never hungry and thirsty, because He provides all of the provisions.

Now, in verse 38 of John 6, Jesus is quoted as saying:

> **For I came down from heaven not to do mine own will, but the will of him that sent me.**

Those words repeat one of the most powerful passages in the Bible, the one in John 5:30, where Jesus says He can do nothing in Himself, but when He hears the Father speaking, He quickly moves. If God said to move to the right, Jesus moved quickly. If the Father said to move to the left, then Jesus moved that way. If God said, go straight, then Jesus went straight ahead.

Be Obedient and Move Quickly

Know the timings of God and be obedient quickly.

Do not allow the adversary to come in and rob, steal, or destroy the Word of God that is being spoken to your spirit.

The Jews began to murmur because they were in spiritual blindness and deafness. They did not understand what He was saying. What does He mean that He is the bread of life come down from heaven?

In verse 48, Jesus made it even plainer in a stronger statement: **I am that bread of life.**

I have a fourteen-year-old son, and if you have, or have had, a teenager, you will know what I mean when I say Jesus made a stronger statement.

I say, "Clarke, pick up your room.

"Yeah, Ma. In a few minutes, Ma.

"Clarke, pick up your room."

"Yeah, Ma. I'm going to do it."

Then, *"Clarke, pick up your room!"*

At that point, he really hears me. And when I read this sixth chapter of John and get to that point, I can almost hear Jesus. He has said it numerous times in different ways:

"I am the bread of life. I came down from heaven. The Father sent Me. I only do His works."

However, in verse 48, that statement is presented by itself. I believe He stood and strongly declared in a ringing voice, "I *am* that bread of life. I am that bread of life!"

> **I am the living bread which came down from heaven: if any man eat of this bread, he shall live for ever; and the bread that I will give is my flesh, which I will give for the life of the world.**
>
> **John 6:51**

All of a sudden, they began to listen, striving among themselves to answer how Jesus could give them *His* flesh to eat. Jesus knew what they were saying and answered them:

> **Then Jesus said unto them, Verily, verily, I say unto you, Except ye eat the flesh of the Son of man, and drink his blood, ye have no life in you.**
>
> **John 6:53**

A few moments before, they had been saying, "Give us this bread. Sure we'll eat it. We want the works of God. We want blind eyes to open, deaf ears to hear, and the dead to be raised."

Jesus had said He was the living bread, the manna from heaven. Now, all of a sudden, He is talking about eating His flesh and drinking His blood. Most of the people around Him at the synagogue in Capernaum when all of this was taking place had seen His works. They had followed Him throughout Galilee.

However, when Jesus plainly began to tell them how they could get the works, they drew back. Many of His disciples went back (looked back, drew back) and followed Him no more, according to John 6:61.

They said, **This is a hard saying; who can hear it?** (v. 60).

The Bible does not tell us what happened to these disciples, and we know that we are not to judge. Actually, we cannot even assume that we know what happened. However, there is the thought within me that it could not possibly have been better for them at the end than at the beginning. They were walking with Jesus, talking with Jesus, eating with Jesus, and seeing the miracles.

Yet, all of a sudden, when continuing to follow Him meant drastic change in their souls, they said, "Hey, nice walking with you, Jesus. I have enjoyed all these months. I have enjoyed seeing the miracles and seeing this power scene. But, listen, I cannot go any farther. This is getting too difficult for me!"

The Word says they walked with Him no more. Somehow, I doubt that the end was better than the beginning. However, I love the way the sixth chapter of John closes.

Jesus turns to the twelve and says, "Aren't you going also?"

And the only one to answer was Peter, who often suffered from hoof-in-mouth disease. Speak before brain gets into gear — that was Peter.

Peter said, "Where would we go? We have followed you this far. You have the words of eternal life. You are the Christ." (v. 68.)

That did not mean Peter and the others would never stumble again. That did not mean they would never fall. There would still be times when it looked as if they had totally missed the mark of the high calling.

But, they said, "No, there really is nothing for us back there. We have forgotten the former things. You are saying to us that a new thing is going to spring forth, and we want to be in on it. We are going to follow You. We may not completely understand. But You said You were the beginning, the end, and the source. So even if we do not understand everything, we will not turn back."

God said, "I am the God whose eyes go to and fro over the whole world. And I have one desire when My eyes go to and fro. That is to show Myself strong on behalf of those whose hearts are blameless." (2 Chron. 15:9.)

So when they determined to follow Jesus, although they did not completely understand, they took a deeper step out into the water. When I was younger, I did the same things as other teenagers. When you step into the water certain times of the year, it is like instant shock! Your entire body below the waist goes numb! But the best way is to jump in. That gets the shock over with all at once. Sometimes that is how we are when we move out in God.

If you will press on in this season of change, regardless of how many times you have fallen, regardless of how many times you have missed the mark, regardless of how many times you have failed in the sight of man and thought you had failed in the sight of God, you can make it. Just do not draw back.

God wants you to win the prize He has set before you more than you do! Why? He wants it because He is not a quitter. He is not a loser, and He does not want His children to be losers or quitters. He is the author *and* the finisher of our faith. He is our source.

In the framework of another sport, I see God as first-base coach. I see Him as third-base coach. I see Him as manager of the team, but I also see Him as pitcher, catcher, and umpire. *He owns the ball*! He owns the bat, and He owns the whole ballpark.

He is saying, "I would not pick a losing team. I would not choose you to be on My team, if I did not know you could make it."

We all have that tendency to look back. But Jesus says, "Don't do that. Don't draw back. With Me, you can make it."

3
Bearing Fruit in the Valley

Whenever there is a new horizon, it always brings forth a new revelation. Whenever there is a time of transition, there is also a time of revelation that comes forth. The Apostle Paul had many horizon experiences.

However, we need to understand that a horizon has limitations. There is a line, or a part, that you cannot see beyond. It looks as if there is no end to it — but there is. The Word of God, from what I have seen and what the Holy Spirit has shown me, shows that you and I can have horizon experiences on a regular basis in Christ Jesus.

Second Corinthians 3:18 tells us that we are transformed from glory to glory. Every time you move from "glory to glory," it is a horizon experience. It is going beyond something you are familiar with to something that has been beyond you up to now. Then a different horizon will be out there in front of you.

There is a story that I tell sometimes that is a very great illustration, a story that is not funny but very graphic. A little boy received a tiny brand new puppy. He went to the grocery store and asked for a box of laundry detergent.

The sales clerk said, "What do you want the box of soap for, son?"

The little boy said, "I want to wash my puppy."

The man said, "Son, this is a very strong detergent, and you have to be very careful. If you are not, you could harm the puppy."

The boy assured the man, "Oh, I'll be very careful. Don't worry!"

Then he went home, opened his mother's washing machine, poured in the soap, and proceeded to put the puppy in the machine. A few days later, he went back into the grocery store, and the man remembered him.

"How's your puppy?" he asked.

"Oh," the little boy said, "my puppy died."

The man exclaimed, "I told you to be careful. That soap is very strong!"

The little boy said, "I don't think it was the soap. I think it was the rinse cycle that killed him."

Transition Is a Rinse Cycle

In a time of transition, many of us feel like we are in a rinse cycle. It seems we are spinning and spinning, and rinsing, and all of this is happening, but we do not know exactly where we are going to come out. During these times, we need to stop and look at how we got into the transition. We need to look back at what happened before the transition began.

In this particular move of the Spirit, we need to look back perhaps over the past ten years and ask ourselves honestly what has happened.

"Where have I been? What have I been doing? What have I accomplished?"

And as we enter this time of transition and honestly answer those questions, our next question should be, "What I am going to do? Where am I *going* from here?"

Most Christians have attended a camp meeting, or a seminar, or a conference at one time or another. During those times, we get all on fire for the Lord. But we have to look at those times as mountain-top experiences, and we need those. However, you cannot live all the time on the mountain top. We *need* times when we gather with other believers and get excited about what God is doing, but then we have to go out and begin to do those works He has shown us.

Recently, as I have been seeking the Lord, I have found that great spiritual leaders of the past had mountain-top experiences, but they never stayed there. Old Testament figures, such as Abraham, Moses, and Elijah, visited God on the mountain top — but they always came down and went to work implementing what God had told them on the mountains. They went up to the mountains to meet God, but they could not remain on the high places. There is nothing wrong with special meetings, but we have to realize those mountain-top experiences are not lasting enough to carry us through the valleys.

Christianity is not a mountain-top experience. Reality in Christianity is life in the valley. It means coming down from the mountain Sunday evening and between Saturday evening of the next week, finding Monday, Tuesday, Wednesday, Thursday, and Friday — the valley. We must learn how to bear fruit in the valley.

God Meets You in the Valley

God does reveal His purpose to us on a mountain top, but much of the time, we are so caught up in the enthusiasm, the excitement, that we do not hear the voice of the Spirit. Where we *really* hear God is in the valleys.

Transition can be a valley experience. I am beginning to see that transition does not necessarily mean being shaken. It does not necessarily mean having to be uprooted.

We know that the day of the "Moses ministry" has passed, and in this new move of the Spirit of God — which I believe began April 1, 1988, and manifested August 1 — we are into a "Joshua ministry." This is the day of possessing the land. We have passed through the day of being promised the land. It is time to possess the land and walk in the valley.

Look at First Samuel 6:13 for a picture of how to bear fruit in the valley.

> **And they of Beth-shemesh were reaping their wheat harvest in the valley: and they lifted up their eyes, and saw the ark, and rejoiced to see it.**

What were they doing in the valley? They were reaping their wheat harvest. Wheat grows in the valley. What grows on the mountain top?

Whenever you fly into the Scandinavian countries or into Switzerland, you fly over the Alps. As you look down and see those peaks, you just pray the plane can go high enough so you do not scrape the bottom!

But what do you see as you look down from the plane? What "grows" on mountain tops? Snow! Lots of snow covers the really high peaks. If the snow melted, which it usually does not, there would be no vegetation. There is no produce, no fruit, nothing that is green. There is nothing alive on top of the highest mountains. Yet Christians are always running after mountain-top experiences. *There is no fruit there.*

The people of Beth-shemesh were harvesting wheat *in the valley.* Something was growing in the valley. The valley had vegetation. It had life. It had fruit.

Many times, mountain-top experiences involve seeking men and not God. Those who attend these special meetings many times are following certain leaders they like. They are seeking ministry or seeking circumstances. When they come out of those meetings — the mountain tops — they bear no fruit. If you go to a seminar because of the charisma of a man or ministry or because of being worked up by religious "razzle dazzle," you will bear no fruit.

However, if you do go to these mountain-top experiences seeking God, you will find Him. If you have not gone up there seeking Jesus, you will be distracted. Our focus needs to be Jesus on the mountain top and Jesus in the valley. Jesus is the author and the finisher of our faith, according to the Word. (Heb. 12:2.) He is our source. He is the one Who will take us up on the mountain and bring us down. He will walk in the valley with us, but only *if we get our eyes off man.*

In First Samuel 6:13, the Word says there was not only a harvest, but one so great it had to be reaped. These people were in the valley reaping the fruit of their labors *and they looked up* to see the Ark and rejoiced.

What Kind of Valley Are You In?

We have seen that the time of growth is in the valley, but we also need to understand that there are different kinds of valleys. The people of Beth-shemesh were in a valley that bore fruit. So there are fruitful valleys, places where growth takes place. But there are the other valleys — valleys of trouble, valleys of weeping, and valleys of decision.

In this time of transition, you are going to have to take an honest look at yourself in order to flow into the next move of the Spirit of God. You are going to have to make an honest decision:

"Why am I here? How did I get here? Is this a valley to bear fruit? Or is this a valley of deception and trouble?"

Deception means not being able to hear God clearly. Many times, deception causes us to be in a situation that looks in the natural like a wilderness or a dry place. To move through the transition into where you are supposed to be requires that you clearly hear what God is saying.

Has God asked you to do something that you are not doing?

Has He told you to go to a person or a place, and you have not?

Has He said to you to support a particular church or ministry, and you are not?

Have you allowed circumstances, situations, and pressures of the world to hinder you?

Any of those things will cause a valley situation in your life.

A word that is not very popular is *repent.* But repenting is necessary to make a transition, to move through the rinse cycle into safety. If you know that you have been in a valley of deception through disobedience, and you want to get out, just repent and pray:

> *"God, I know You asked me to do a certain thing. I know You told me to go to a certain place, or to say a certain thing, or to give a certain amount of money. Now I realize, Father, that because I have not been obedient, my life has been in a valley with no hope. I have only looked at the sacrifice and not at obedience. God, I am sorry."*

After you have repented and committed to obey, then make a 180-degree turn, and press on with God. This is a time to allow one's heart to be circumcised by obedience and purity, by doing what God has told you to do.

4
There Are Springs in the Valleys

In this chapter, I want to talk about two kinds of valleys: the valleys of trouble and weeping. I particularly want you to notice that in any of the valleys, *there are springs* if you look to God.

In Hosea 2, God was speaking to Israel, who had been unfaithful. He was warning through His prophet that He was about to take Israel into a spiritual Valley of Achor as a transition from the days of disobedience and bondage to false gods. *Achor* means "trouble, or affliction."[1]

Israel figuratively had gone back into Egypt through its lifestyle and paganism. In the Valley of Achor, God said, Israel would be given a vineyard.

> **Therefore, behold, I will allure her, and bring her into the wilderness,**
>
> **And I will give her vineyards from thence, and the valley of Achor for a door of hope: and she shall sing there, as in the days of her youth, and as in the day when she came up out of the land of Egypt.**
>
> **Hosea 2:14,15**

You may say, "I do not want to go into any wilderness! Stop right there. Don't allure me into any wilderness by speaking comfortably to me."

[1] Packer, J. L.; Tenney, Merrill C.; White, William, Jr. *The Bible Almanac* (Nashville: Thomas Nelson Publishers, 1980), p. 681.

Many times Christians feel that God is not in the wilderness. To my knowledge. God is everywhere. He is omnipresent and omniscient (all-knowing). He is on the mountain top, in the valley, and in the wilderness. He is over the horizon and in the transition period.

Notice that Hosea said God would give Israel a vineyard. A vineyard is a place where fruit grows. The valleys are the places where fruit grows. In our lives, when we come down from the mountain tops in obedience, God will create vineyards within our valleys. Vineyards produce grapes, and wine is made from grapes. God will bring forth a new wine in your valley, the wine of the Holy Spirit.

However, in order to get wine, there must be pressure. Many times, it takes pressure to produce the fruit within our valleys.

God was going to take Israel into a transition period — a valley of trouble, a valley of affliction. But notice that this valley was to be *a door of hope.* Many times, we have our eyes so fixed on the trouble that we cannot see the hope. We cannot see that this transition period, this valley, is leading us to somewhere else.

You have come down from the mountain. You are in a valley, when all of a sudden, there is a door of hope! You cannot just keep your eyes on the valley — the trouble — although the fruit is coming forth under pressure. You must keep your eyes on Jesus, Who is your door of hope.

David went through many pressures. Many of our well-loved psalms were the fruits of the pressure put on David during valleys of trouble in his life. In Psalm 27:13, he responded to pressure by saying:

> **I had fainted unless I had believed to see the goodness of the Lord in the land of the living.**

He did not say *the goodness of the Lord* in the land of the dead, or the land of the barren where no fruit, no produce, comes forth. Every one of us is in the land of the living. We are not in the land of the dead.

Look again at Hosea 2.

> **And it shall be at that day, saith the Lord,** (What day? The day you come into the wilderness, the day He will speak to you "comfortably.") **that thou shalt call me Ishi; and shalt call me no more Baali.** (Meaning, "You will call me husband, and no longer call me master.")
>
> **For I will take away the names of Baalim out of her mouth, and they shall no more be remembered by their name.**
>
> **And in that day will I make a covenant for them with the beasts of the field, and with the fowls of heaven, and with the creeping things of the ground: and I will break the bow and the sword and the battle out of the earth, and will make them to lie down safely.**
>
> **And I will betroth thee unto me for ever; yea, I will betroth thee unto me in righteousness, and in judgment, and in lovingkindness, and in mercies.**
>
> **Hosea 2:16-19**

Growth Requires Water

To bear fruit a valley must have certain things. It must have good soil — a born again spirit and renewed mind in which to work. Also, the valley must have enough water.

To see another truth, let us switch metaphors and consider a "harvest" of sheep instead of grains or fruit.

If you have ever spent any time on a farm or ranch, you will know that you cannot take sheep around a babbling brook. The noise of fast water or water running over rocks and debris will "spook" them. You have to take sheep by quiet, still streams to give them water for their thirst. You have to water them in the peaceful places.

In those verses in Hosea, God said that if Israel would seek Him in the Valley of Achor, He would cause that place of trouble or affliction to become a place in which they could lie down in peace and rest.

Spiritually, we can apply those verses to us today. If we seek Him in the valleys, He will make us places to rest *even in the midst of trouble.*

How can that be done? You can find that place of rest if you look at Jesus and not at the trouble, look to your Father and not *at* circumstances. Look for favor from on high while you are in the valleys.

Consider transitional periods when things seem rocky to be doors of hope. God will bring you out the other side better than ever and ready to bear much fruit, *if you will let Him.*

Another prophet talked about the Valley of Achor, and that was Isaiah. Again, God was speaking to His people. This time, He was talking to Judah in the time of the divided kingdoms. Israel had already been carried off into Assyrian captivity, a big-time valley of trouble. Now Judah was approaching the same degree of spiritual adultery and idolatry. Judah was moving into the place where God would take her into her own valley of trouble.

Also, in this passage, God was looking ahead some six hundred years to the time when His Son would come out of Judah.

> **Your iniquities, and the iniquities of your fathers together, saith the Lord, which have burned incense upon the mountains, and blasphemed me upon the hills: therefore will I measure their former work into their bosom.**
>
> **Thus saith the Lord, As the new wine is found in the cluster, and one saith, Destroy it not; for a blessing is in it: so will I do for my servants' sakes, that I may not destroy them all.**
>
> **And I will bring forth a seed out of Jacob, and out of Judah an inheritor of my mountains: and mine elect shall inherit it, and my servants shall dwell there.**
>
> **And Sharon shall be a fold of flocks, and the valley of Achor a place for the herds to lie down in, for my people that have sought me.**
>
> **Isaiah 65:7-10**

God was saying that in Jesus the valleys of trouble could become a place to rest, a place to lie down **for my people that have sought me.** That last phrase is the key to whether valleys of affliction or trouble actually become doors of hope.

Seek God in the valleys. Look upward! See the Ark, and rejoice. (1 Sam. 6:13.) Look for favor from God in the valleys. Do not look for trouble or at trouble. Those valleys can be a place of inheritance, a place where the door of hope leads to blessings.

Matthew wrote:

> **But seek ye first the kingdom of God, and his righteousness; and all these things shall be added unto you.**
>
> **Matthew 6:33**

When you seek God in the valley, He will make it a place of rest.

Let us look now at a different type of valley that is mentioned in the Word. This one is found in Psalms.

A Valley of Weeping

Psalm 84 talks about a valley of weeping. Have you ever spent any time in the valley of weeping? Have you ever wept before the Lord? There are different kinds of weeping: weeping in the flesh, out of the fleshly emotions; weeping in prayer before the Lord, and weeping with other people for their sake. The psalmist wrote:

> **Blessed is the man whose strength is in thee; in whose heart are the ways of them.**
>
> **Who passing through the valley of Baca** (weeping) **make it a well; the rain also filleth the pools.**
>
> **They go from strength to strength, every one of them in Zion appeareth before God.**
>
> **Psalm 84:5-7**

The first thing to note is that the people this psalm is talking about are not *staying* in the valley. They are *passing through* this valley. But what are you supposed to do as you pass through a valley of weeping (no matter what kind of weeping it is)? *You are to make this valley into a well!*

Make a well, and the rain will fill the pools. Then this valley can become a fruitful place, a place where things can grow. Instead of crying out, "Oh, woe is me," make a well. Instead of saying, "Oh, God. I'm the only one left," as Elijah did, make a well. Elijah was looking at his own circumstances, when really God had seven thousand more prophets who had not gone over to the worship of Baal. (1 Kings 19:18.) Do not look at your own circumstances in a valley of weeping. Do the same thing as in the other valleys: look upward at the Ark (Jesus) and rejoice.

God said, "Make a well, and I will fill it with rain."

Another way of saying this is found in Isaiah 55:1.

> **Ho, every one that thirsteth, come ye to the waters, and he that hath no money; come ye, buy, and eat; yea, come, buy wine and milk without money and without price.**

What do you do in the valley of dryness and thirstiness, the valley of weeping? You go to God.

God is not asking you for anything but is saying to you, "If you are thirsty, if you are dry, come unto me. Come to me, and I will cause a refreshing in you. I will cause a revitalization to come into you. I will cause nourishment to come into you. Don't look at this time of weeping, but make it a well, in order that I can fill it with the refreshing waters of my Spirit."

Psalm 104:10-13 says:

> **He sendeth the springs into the valleys, which run among the hills.**
>
> **They give drink to every beast of the field: the wild asses quench their thirst.**
>
> **By them shall the fowls of the heaven have their habitation, which sing among the branches.**
>
> **He watereth the hills from his chambers: the earth is satisfied with the fruit of thy works.**

If you look to God, He will send His springs in your valleys and cause you to be a refreshing to other people.

In Isaiah 41:18, God spoke these words through the prophet:

> **I will open rivers in high places, and fountains in the midst of the valleys: I will make the wilderness a•pool of water, and the dry land springs of water.**

Do you have faith?

You might say, "Well, I can believe God for a little spring in this valley."

But God is saying, "I will not only give you a spring, but I will cause fountains to spring forth. I will bring forth fountains of living water. There will not be a time of dryness in this valley."

5
The Valley of Decision

Transition periods usually are valleys of decision, and most of us are there today as part of the Church. This *is* a time of decision for the Body of Christ. Valleys of decision mean the day of the Lord is near, at least in a spiritual sense. Joel 3:14 talks about multitudes being in the valley of decision.

> **Multitudes, multitudes in the valley of decision: for the day of the Lord is near in the valley of decision.**

Most of us have come up out of the land of Egypt, which is the type and shadow of sin. We have been born again. If you are born again, you are no longer in darkness. You have been delivered. You have been transferred into the Kingdom of God's dear Son. Egypt is no longer part and parcel of you. Egypt no longer has a legal right to take hold of you when you have been delivered by the Son of God.

In spite of having been delivered out of Egypt, does it feel as if you are still there? Sometimes the transition periods are more like a wilderness than like a valley. If you are in disobedience, it may take a wilderness experience to bring you through the transition from being delivered into the valleys of the Promised Land where you can bear fruit.

But we saw in the last chapter that if you look to God, He will cause fountains to spring up in your wilderness. During such a time, you need to ask yourself these questions:

What is my call?

Where is my place?

Am I in the position where God wants me in His Body?

Am I willing, during this time of transition, to remain in the permissive will of God?

Or am I going to make a quality decision once and for all to stop merely confessing with my mouth and move out to act on the Word?

Am I willing to choose the pressure or the sacrifice necessary to move on into the perfect will of God and bear fruit?

We want God to make all our decisions, tell us what to do, and make our plans. We almost want Him to cook our meals, spiritually speaking. Most of the time, He has already spoken. The reason we are in the valley of decision is because we have not decided to act on what He has told us. We have not taken the time to listen.

Many times, when we are faced with decisions, we want the loud, booming voice of God to tell us exactly what to do. But our free wills are involved. He can tell us, but the decision to do it *must* be ours.

Listen to the Still, Small Voice

Earlier, I mentioned Elijah's times of decision when Jezebel threatened to kill him in retaliation for the deaths of her prophets. Even after the great miracles God had done through him — no rain for three and a half years, the fire which burned up even the stones of the altar during the confrontation with the priests of Baal, and the great victory over those priests — when Jezebel said she was going to kill him, Elijah ran in fear.

First Kings 19 relates what happened. Elijah ran into the wilderness, sat down under a juniper tree, and begged God to take his life for he was not any better than his "fathers." (v. 4.) You know he did not mean it. He did not want God to kill him. If he really wanted to die, he could have stayed near the palace in Samaria, and Jezebel would have taken care of that for him! So you know he lied.

It was easier to say, "God, kill me. God, You become a murderer so I can be a martyr and look good."

But the Lord sent an angel to feed him. The angel baked a cake and provided a pitcher of water, and fed him two meals. That cake kept him going for forty days and nights. During that time, Elijah found a cave to live in.

There, the Lord spoke to him and said, "Elijah, what are you doing here?" (v. 9.)

> **And he said, I have been very jealous for the Lord God of hosts: for the children of Israel have forsaken thy covenant, thrown down thine altars, and slain thy prophets with the sword; and I, even I only, am left; and they seek my life, to take it away.**
>
> **And he** (the Lord) **said, Go forth, and stand upon the mount before the Lord. And, behold, the Lord passed by, and a great and strong wind rent the mountains, and brake in pieces the rocks**

> **before the Lord; but the Lord was not in the wind: and after the wind an earthquake; but the Lord was not in the earthquake:**
>
> **And after the earthquake a fire; but the Lord was not in the fire: and after the fire a still small voice.**
>
> **1 Kings 19:10-12**

Elijah was in a valley of decision. The cave where he had hidden became a place of transition. Either he hid from Jezebel for the rest of his life, or he would come back out stronger than ever.

Then God said, "Come out of that cave and stand before me."

Elijah said, "Here I am, Lord. How come I do not hear any wind? How come I do not hear any thunder? If it is really You speaking to me, there should at least be fire. How about shaking the cave a little bit, God? Just so I'll know it's really you."

However, the Word says that God was not in the earthquake, the wind, or the fire. He was a still, small voice.

Many times, when we are faced with decisions, we want the loud, booming voice of God to speak to us, to tell us what to do.

"God, *You* tell me what to do. Show me what to do."

However, most of the time, God has already spoken. We have not taken the time or made the effort to hear. We are too busy looking at the trouble to hear His still, small voice.

Keep Digging in the Valley

Look at Genesis 26:19:

And Isaac's servants digged in the valley, and found there a well of springing water.

So what did Elijah need to do? What do we need to do? We need to "dig in the valley" until we find that spring, that fountain of water springing forth. That is how you find the door of hope. You must dig and dig until you find the water. Until you find the answer in God, continue digging in the valley.

If you need a healing, what are you going to do? Walk around saying, "Well, I just don't know if I'll ever be healed, or not? I don't know if I'll ever be restored."

No, the Word says to dig, dig, dig, until you find the water. John 7:38 says that out of your belly shall flow rivers of living water. You keep digging.

How do you dig? You dig for the water through prayer. You dig for the fountain through fasting. You dig by making changes in your attitudes. You dig by throwing off fear and becoming willing to do what God has asked you to do. If you believe God, and trust Him, *you will hit water in that valley.*

Some time ago, I was ministering in Atlanta, Georgia, at a camp meeting and teaching on the presence of the Lord. This was one of those times when everything came together in spiritual unity: the music was right, the worship was right, and the anointing was heavy. Everything meshed together in the Spirit. All of the elements of the service were right for the Holy Spirit to manifest, and the atmosphere was electrifying.

As the ministry went forth, there was a strong anointing for healing and deliverance. The word of knowledge came forth that there were people there with terminal illnesses. Several people who had cancer came up to be prayed for. Then I noticed two men walking over to the platform. Probably a thousand people were there, and many were coming up to be prayed for from all over the building. But I noticed these two in particular.

Just from looking at them in the natural, I knew one young man was dying of AIDS. As I leaned down from the platform, some of my intercessors were praying around me. There was a strong anointing also for deliverance.

Both of the young men told me they were in advanced stages of AIDS, although only one's illness was obvious to the natural eye. We prayed for them to be healed, and after the meeting ended, I went on with my schedule. Somehow, in the months following, the face of the young man whose illness was not as obvious came before me again and again.

I did not know if he was alive. I did not know if he was dead. I did not even know his name or where he was from, but I continued to pray for him.

A year later, I was back at the same camp meeting, and on the second day as I walked out to get lunch with a friend, I looked out of the corner of my eye — and there was that young man!

He came up and said, "Valerie, do you remember me?"

I said, "Do I remember *you!* Your face has been before me many times. I didn't know if you were alive or what happened to you, but I have held you up in prayer."

He said, "Do you remember that you prayed for me for AIDS?"

I answered yes, and he said, "I was in the advanced stages, Valerie, but I have been to the doctor. And there is no more AIDS!"

He was totally healed, totally delivered by the power of God.

Do not tell me he was not in a valley! But he kept digging and digging and found the well. He brought others to be prayed for at that second camp meeting, one of them a very young boy who is an AIDS carrier. He had lived as a homosexual for four years, but for the past two years, he had been born again.

I put my arms around the young boy, Kenny, and he said, "Aren't you afraid to touch me?"

I told him no, and I held him in my arms for quite a while.

He said, "I don't understand it. I have been kicked out of three churches because they found out I was an AIDS carrier. My parents have made a separate wing in our home with a private bath for me, because they are afraid to touch anything. I have my own dishes, my own glassware, even my own dishwasher. Why aren't you afraid to touch me?"

The only thing I could answer was what the Spirit of God had told me and my workers in Poland during the Chernobal disaster. We were in that area during the whole time of the incident and the resulting fallout.

When we got home, people said, "You need to go and get some tests run, because you have been exposed to radiation.

But the Holy Spirit quickened to us that the glory of God is a consuming fire, and that the glory of God within us was greater than any fallout. That was the only thing I could tell this young man:

"I don't have a fear to hug you. I am not afraid to touch you, because the glory of God is a consuming fire."

I prayed for him, and I trust that we will be hearing from him shortly. Man, Church, and ministries have said a person can never be cured of AIDS. I have heard too many ministers say that. *But nothing is impossible with God.*

Kenny could look right next to himself and see with his own eyes someone who had been "cured" of AIDS, totally healed and verified by medical reports. That was a door of hope in his valley.

So no matter what kind of valley you are in, keep digging!

The Church Is in a Valley of Decision

I have found that there is a direct relationship between every trial, every valley situation, and the release of the anointing in your life. The more trials, the more wilderness experiences, the more valley times you come through spiritually successful, the stronger the anointing is in your life. The anointing is freely given, a manifestation of the Holy Spirit. But it takes digging and digging to be able to find that well in your spirit from which the anointing springs forth.

There has been a Valley of Achor for the Church, a valley of weeping. Now there is a valley to stop and make Christians think. Most Christians today are in a valley of decision, I believe. This is a time of decision. It is a time when the Spirit of God has been moving in a forceful way.

We hear from many ministers that the day of "playing church" is over. We have clapped and cheered and shouted.

We have said, "Yes, Amen. Brother, preach it."

However, it is time to get serious. God is calling out His troops, and the pressure is on. Our gentle Holy Spirit has become forceful.

He is saying, "Church, this is a time of decision. This is a time to know that you know that you know that the Lord is your shepherd. David said in Psalm 27:13 that he would have fainted if he had not believed in the goodness of the Lord. This is a time to get the goodness of the Lord solidly in our hearts.

The Lord is my shepherd; I shall not want.

He maketh me to lie down in green pastures: he leadeth me beside the still waters.

He restoreth my soul: he leadeth me in the paths of righteousness for his name's sake.

> **Yea, though I walk through the valley of the shadow of death** (There is yet another type of valley!), **I will fear no evil: for thou art with me; thy rod and thy staff they comfort me.**
>
> **Thou preparest a table before me in the presence of mine enemies: thou anointest my head with oil; my cup runneth over.**
>
> **Surely goodness and mercy shall follow me all the days of my life: and I will dwell in the house of the Lord for ever.**
>
> **Psalm 23:1-6**

The Lord *is* our shepherd, and there has never been a shepherd who loved his flock and took them to troubled waters. A good shepherd always brings the flock to a place of rest. Even in the Valley of Achor, the Lord will cause you to lie down and rest. He will restore your soul and make a path of righteousness for you. He will walk with you through all of the valleys, including the valley of death.

Seek God, not man, so that when you come down from the mountain tops of camp meetings, seminars, and special meetings, your Shepherd will be with you in the valleys of life. He will comfort you. *Life is a valley situation.*

Jesus will prepare a table for you in the presence of your enemies. He will anoint your head with oil. During this time of transition, this valley of decision, the Holy Spirit has not stopped pouring forth His fresh oil. He pours it forth every single day so that your cup can run over. How do I know? Because He said His goodness and mercy would follow you all the days of your life.

Keep digging, and believe that God wants you to hit the water He has provided for you in this valley.

6
A Change Is Coming

The Apostle Paul wrote to the church at Corinth:

> **I have planted, Apollos watered; but God gave the increase.**
>
> **So then neither is he that planteth any thing, neither he that watereth; but God that giveth the increase.**
>
> **Now he that planteth and he that watereth are one: and every man shall receive his own reward according to his own labour.**
>
> **For we are labourers together with God: ye are God's husbandry, ye are God's building.**
>
> **According to the grace of God which is given unto me, as a wise masterbuilder, I have laid the foundation, and another buildeth thereon. But let every man take heed how he buildeth thereupon.**
>
> **For other foundation can no man lay than that is laid, which is Christ Jesus.**
>
> **1 Corinthians 3:6-11**

Mountain-top experiences, such as conventions, seminars, and so forth, can be like changes in architectural designs — if you go to them determined to receive truth from God, no matter what it means in your life. If you go following a person, or for "experiences," or for other soulish reasons, you will receive no revelation in your heart, and there will be no changes in your life. You will come down from the mountain with the same old design in your lifestyle.

We fear change, because sometimes it can be painful. However, it is not necessary for change always to hurt. If you *yield* to the change, things will be a lot easier and less painful. Usually, the pain comes because you are fighting whatever the change is.

Change Does Not Have To Be Painful

My grandmother prophesied how she would die. Even the change of death does not have to be painful.

She said, "Valerie, when I die, I do not want you to cry, because I am only going to leave here to continue doing up in heaven what I do here."

My grandmother was a master hand at growing flowers and working in the garden.

She told me, "When I die, I'm even going to die in my rose bed. Then you'll understand that I'm just going to go from here and continue working up there."

And that is exactly how she died. She was a very wise person.

However, when I was very young, I did not think she was so wise, especially when she would have my cousin and me stand before her periodically and take a tablespoonful of castor oil and a tablespoonful of cod liver oil.

She spoke Polish and refused to speak English. So until I was twenty-one, when she died, I never heard a word of English out of her. She spoke English to all my friends but not to me. If I tried to speak to her in English, she instantly went deaf. She would not receive it from me. So when I would plead with her in English that I did not need the doses of oil and could not see any need of my taking them, she would not "hear" me.

Although I could not see the need for the oil, it was good for me. We may not see the need for changes, that sometimes approach us as if God were holding out a spoonful of castor oil, but whatever it is will be good for us — or God would not bring it. When changes are ordained by the Holy Spirit according to God's master plan, they do not have to be painful. Just take it quickly and get it over with. Then we will see the results in our well-being.

In Romans 1:1, Paul wrote that he was a servant of Jesus, who was separated as an apostle unto the good news of God. The word *separated* there is *aphorzio*,[1] which really is two words: aph, "away from," and *horzio*, "horizon." It means "to mark off by bounds," "to limit." Paul, the servant of Jesus Christ and called to be an apostle, was *set apart*. A horizon so often marks a boundary, a limitation.

We in the Body of Christ have been separated from the limited horizon of this world and given an unlimited horizon. When we were in the natural world, our lives were limited. But once Christ is established in our lives, no longer is there a limit to our horizons. No longer is there a limit to what God has planned for us.

---

[1]Vine, W. E. *Vine's Expository Dictionary of Old and New Testament Words* (Old Tappan: Fleming Revell Company, Copyright (C) 1981), p. 345, Vol. 3.

God is the Master Builder, the designer of a master plan. But He says that it is up to us how we build. We can follow His blueprint, and He knows how to make it come into line. Or we can choose to follow our own blueprints and build on shaky foundations.

Actually, Paul had three different types of separation:

He was separated to God from his mother's womb. (Gal. 1:5.)

He was separated by God as a *chosen vessel.* (Acts 9:15.)

He was separated as an apostle. (Acts 13:2.)

There is a difference between a vessel of honor and a vessel of dishonor. A *chosen vessel* is a vessel of honor. Even today, if you visited a potter in a Middle Eastern country and asked for a "chosen vessel," he would choose the finest piece of pottery from a selection of fine pieces, and sign his name to it. No matter where the piece of pottery was found, it would always bring honor to the potter.

Paul was saying he had an inscription upon him from God designating him a *chosen vessel.* So do we! Like Paul, every born again child of God is a *chosen vessel*, separated from his or her mother's womb. Some of us are called into one of the fivefold offices. Others are not, but *all* are called into certain portions of the Body of Christ. All of us should be living so that we do not bring reproach on the name of our potter, Jesus.

Every Christian has a specific role, a specific function, in the Body.

New Horizons Bring New Revelations

Revelation knowledge is being loosed upon the Church today.

People often say, "Yes, but there is nothing new under heaven." (Eccl. 1:9.)

But Ephesians 3:5 says the mystery of the Gospel was not disclosed in the past **as it is now in this generation revealed unto his holy apostles and his prophets.** Today, more revelation of the mysteries of the Word are being revealed to His people. These things are not new in the sense of "original," but they are new to us. They have been in the Word all of the time, but we have not had the understanding of them.

God is wanting to increase the capacity in every one of us to take in His revelations.

Often, we hear the expression, "Oh, if I could just be like a pipe. If I could just be an instrument and have the Holy Spirit flow through me."

God does not want you to be a "pipe." There is a vast difference between a vessel and a pipe. A vessel contains the liquid and pours it out as needed. God wants to increase our capacities. He wants us to come before Him so that He can expound revelation upon revelation.

For too long, members of the Body of Christ have warmed the pews and allowed the fivefold ministries to pour things down upon their heads. If we, who are in those ministries, have trained the Body to sit there and receive, but not go before the Lord for themselves, then we have erred. You have the same Holy Spirit whom I have in me. Seeking God for His understanding, discernment, or revelation is not taking away from the anointing. It does not take away from the offices set in the Church.

God wants to reveal Himself to each of us, and we will never have a revelation of who we are until we get a revelation of who He is. You can listen to all of the tapes and all of the sermons, but until you come to *know* Him for yourself, you will only know Him second-hand through the experiences of the speakers.

In a new horizon, I believe we are lifted up into a new dimension. If conferences, seminars, or camp meetings do not cause stirrings within us, then I believe we have ceased to bring forth the result God wants. If a meeting does not bring forth something you can walk out of the door with, then the time has been wasted. You should walk out of every service with something for the future.

You should be able to go to God and say, "Father, I have received something of You. Now I want you to increase it in me until it causes a change in my life."

So often in late years, we have talked about a new wave. But do you know that some Christians are going to miss it? The reason is because *a new wave* means change. It means people are going to have to accept something different, and more than likely, change some of the things they believed or took for granted.

Change Is an Earthly Name For the School of the Holy Spirit

The Holy Spirit quickened this thought to me, "Change is an earthly name, or description, of the School of the Holy Spirit."

Safety never comes in the Christian experience from the absence of danger, but safety comes from the presence of God. Change may mean danger to our traditions, our lifestyles, our attitudes and behavior, and our ways. But safety, when God brings us a revelation that means change, comes from submitting to His will and allowing His will to be accomplished. The real danger to our spiritual lives is in refusing to submit to His changes.

Psalm 31:20 says that He will hide us in His presence from the strife of tongues and the pride of man. That verse does not say that we will not have prideful men coming against us. It does not say that tongues will not be used against us. In spite of those things, however, we have safety in the presence of God.

When my son was small, He fell before he was two years old and cut his forehead so badly it needed stitches. Then he fell and got a cut over his eye and needed stitches. Then he broke his finger.

At that point, I said, "There is no way I am going to take him to the hospital. John, you take him. They are going to think I am abusing this child!"

If there were any way, I would have rounded off every corner in the house. I would have taken out the coffee table. I would have taken out the fireplace. But I could not remove all the possible obstacles. Clarke had to learn to walk around them. Yes, he fell, but there came a time when he did learn to walk properly. He learned how to manuever around obstacles.

There was no safety in a lack of danger for him. If we had kept him in a padded room, he never would have learned to walk and live in the real world. His safety was in the presence of his parents, who could pick him up, comfort him, and rush him to the hospital if necessary. It takes patience to learn to walk a new pathway.

Patience Takes Discipline

On one of my ministry visits to California, I was in an area noted for surfing, and I walked out on the beach to watch. I noticed that some people immediately jumped up whenever a wave rolled in. They ran out on their surfboards and got on that wave.

But there were others sitting there who did not move on every wave. I found they were the experienced surfers. The amateur surfers — maybe they had just gotten their boards for Christmas — would try to ride every wave. That way, they got on lesser waves, and many times that would cause them to miss the big wave coming in. The experienced surfer knows to wait, which takes discipline.

Can you imagine sitting there and seeing what

looks like a great wave to ride, but because of past experience, you know better?

You wait because you have trained yourself to sit for hours if necessary and watch for the big one. It is worth waiting for rather than exhaust yourself on lesser waves.

There is a change coming in the Body, and we need to learn to wait for it rather than ride lesser waves.

If you had walked a certain pathway all your life, you could cover your eyes and probably still walk it. You would have become familiar with it even in darkness. But then suppose you have to walk a different path. There would be new obstacles, new rocks, and new twists and turns to take. If you did not watch where you were going, you would stumble.

During change, many times there are stumbling blocks. I believe we are coming into the greatest move of God on the face of the earth, one which will require change and which will consequently have new paths to learn, new stones in the path to deal with. If we do not know where those stones are, we will stumble over them.

Something which seems to be a stumbling block to many are the vessels through which new messages emerge. Often, there is an unwillingness to accept the vessel, the means by which the new message is brought. God brings people forth in a new pathway, people who have an understanding of what His purpose is at the time of the new wave. They are not always accepted.

Every change of God also is accompanied by new signs and wonders. Those things can be a rock to those who do not want to change. The nineteenth century Church stumbled over tongues in the beginning of the Pentecostal movement. When the Charismatic movement began, Pentecostals did not like them. Many Christians made stumbling blocks out of them, when they should have been joining them in change. Every time God adds another section of His master plan, there will be new signs accompanying it.

Another area that could turn into a stumbling block is His purpose in the new move. His new message is not always accepted. So we see three areas of change that can be stumbling blocks to people: the vessels being used, the different kinds of signs, and the overall purpose of God.

For example, suppose God chose to use all very young people, and those youngsters came forth and brought a message. How many Christians would be looking at their age and not listening with the eyes of their spirits?

How many would say, "You don't have enough wisdom to teach me. How dare you say that to me?"

Three Kinds of Strength

Isaiah 40 talks about three different types of strength, and it takes strength to ride spiritual waves just as it takes strength to ride ocean waves. For those experienced in riding the waves of the Holy Spirit, those who are waiting patiently for the big wave to come in, spiritual strength is the key.

O Zion, that bringest good tidings, get thee up into the high mountain; O Jerusalem, that bringest good tidings, lift up thy voice with strength; lift it up, be not afraid; say unto the cities of Judah, Behold your God!

Isaiah 40:9

This verse is talking about a strength *to endure.* The prophet was saying to lift up your voices with strength. But there is a second kind of strength found in verse 26.

Lift up your eyes on high, and behold who hath created these things, that bringeth out their host by number: he calleth them all by names by the greatness of his might, for that he is *strong in power;* not one faileth.

This verse is talking about the strength of the Lord. He knows all of His hosts by name, and He knows that in the strength of His power not one will be lost. That word *ammitz* translated *strength* means "actively working."[2] There is yet another type of strength found in that chapter.

He giveth power to the faint; and to them that have no might, he increaseth strength.

Isaiah 40:9,26,29

This verse is talking about strength for your defense. Not only will God give us strength to lift up our voices and endure, and strength to actively work, but He gives us strength for our defense.

However, there is a key to how these strengths are received, and it is right at the end of that chapter not in the beginning.

---

[2] *The Companion Bible* (Grand Rapids: Zondervan Bible Publishers, 1974), p. 981.

> **But they that *wait* upon the Lord shall renew their strength; they shall mount up with wings as eagles; they shall run, and not be weary; and they shall walk, and not faint.**
>
> **Isaiah 40:31**

The key is *to wait upon the Lord*. Those who wait will renew their strength.

Psalm 27:14 also says:

> **Wait on the Lord: be of good courage, and he shall strengthen thine heart: wait, I say, on the Lord.**

And Proverbs 20:22 says:

> **...Wait on the Lord, and he shall save thee.**

It takes discipline to wait on the Lord — at least, it does for me! I want God to do everything yesterday. I have heard about miracles and works that we are going to do, but finally I became "sick and tired" of hearing about what God was *going* to do. I went before the Lord and said, "I don't understand!" But for some reason, Psalm 27:14 keeps coming up in my spirit: **Wait on the Lord ...wait, I say, on the Lord.**

I do not want to wait, but I am learning. I am learning that it takes discipline to bring about change.

We have a high calling. The Church age is not over. I believe we are coming into a newness in that age, and we are going to learn what "Kingdom living" is here on earth. Paul wrote to the Ephesians a prayer that is still valid for us today.

> **That the God of our Lord Jesus Christ, the Father of glory, may give unto you the spirit of wisdom and revelation in the knowledge of him:**

> **The eyes of your understanding being enlightened; that ye may know what is the hope of his calling, and what the riches of the glory of his inheritance in the saints.**
>
> **Ephesians 1:17,18**

How do you receive a spirit of wisdom and revelation that deepens your knowledge of Jesus? You receive that revelation from the Holy Spirit by having the eyes of your understanding flooded with light, in order that you may understand the hope into which He has called you. There is a high calling (Phil. 3:14), a hope, that I think we have not understood clearly in the past. We have stumbled over the new moves of God. The Church has fallen because of a lack of understanding, as well as a lack of knowledge.

I pray for wisdom all of the time, but I also pray for understanding. You can pray this prayer:

> *"Lord, give me understanding so that I know what You want me to know. There is a mark of the high calling that You have placed before me. You have placed it before the Body in general, but You also have placed a specific calling before me. You said that if I pray to You, the God of glory, I would receive wisdom and revelation and understanding on how to reach for the hope of that high calling."*

Psalm 103:7 says:

> **He made known his ways to Moses, his acts unto the children of Israel.**

Learn the Ways of God

Our highest goal should be to know the ways of God, not just the acts of God — as I pointed out earlier in this book. So often we run after what God is doing and do not seek to know Who He really is. Do not just be a follower of His acts, be one who works in His ways.

It is not enough to get excited during meetings, or during a service. You should have a new excitement about knowing God rising up in you every day. Knowing His ways will cause that sense of anticipation for what He is going to do next to arise constantly within you.

Do you know God wants to use you?

Do you know God loves you?

Do you know God is not a loser?

Do you know God has never chosen a loser? He does not have a losing team. He is not stupid.

God is not going to call you to do something and then say, "Boy, I blew that one! What a turkey I picked."

He knows the end results. He knows what you can do, if you will. He knows your potential. But it is up to you, and to me, to get into the ways of God. God has confidence in us, a lot more than we have in ourselves. So often, we get our eyes on the experience. We get our eyes on the moment instead of on the development of what God is doing in our lives.

I have done that before. I have gotten my eyes on the experience. By having my eyes on the moment, I lost sight of what God was doing in my life. I did not see the development of character that God was trying to establish. That is why we must keep our eyes on the process of that development and on what He is building.

The real character, the real test of character, of a mature person is revealed in who he is in the dark.

7
The Refining Process of God

One reason many Christians are having difficulty accepting this period of transition is that the Church has grown complacent during the past decades. When Zion becomes complacent, she is no different than any other group, or individual, she becomes stagnant and stale. The first-hand revelations become second-hand revelations, which are never fresh and exciting.

In the Church today, there are too many Christians who do not want change in their lives. They do not want the taste of new wine the Holy Spirit is trying to bring to them.

In this chapter, we are going to talk a little about vessels, but the emphasis is not on the vessel so much as on the wine. God spoke about the process of making wine when He pronounced judgment on the country of Moab, the place where the book of Ruth begins.

The book of Ruth is a book of transition. It was written about something that happened during the time when judges ruled the united monarchy of Israel. The first chapter of Ruth is about three women in a valley of decision: Naomi, and her daughters-in-law, Orpah and Ruth.

Naomi knew it was time to get back to the place where God was. She had been living in Moab with her husband and two sons, who had died. She made a decision to go back to the Promised Land, and one daughter-in-law started with her, but turned back. Remember what happens to those who turn back? At any rate, this daughter-in-law is never mentioned again. She no longer had any part in what God was doing, *because she turned back.*

The other daughter, Ruth, made her mother-in-law's God *her* God and moved into an important place in God's plan through her obedience. She became the great-grandmother of David and an ancestor of Jesus, although she was not a native Israelite but a Moabite and descended from a people born out of incest. Ruth allowed God to bring about drastic changes in her life. She made a new beginning out of her valley of decision.

However, the main thing I want you to see about the country of Moab is found in Jeremiah hundreds of years later when Israel had divided into two nations. The Nation of Israel already had gone into exile, and God was beginning to deal with the Nation of Judah before sending the Jews into exile in Babylon. At the same time, He was dealing with surrounding nations as well. His day of judgment was about to fall on the entire Palestinian area, but this particular chapter is directed to Moab.

> **Moab hath been at ease from his youth, and he hath settled on his lees, and hath not been emptied from vessel to vessel, neither hath he gone into captivity: therefore his taste remained in him, and his scent is not changed.**
>
> **Jeremiah 48:11**

In other words, Moab was well on the way to becoming stale and stagnant. Moab was a portion of the Middle East that grew some of the finest grapes from which some of the finest wines were produced.

Wine Is Poured From Vessel to Vessel

Esther 1:7 says the guests of the king were given drink **in vessels of gold, (the vessels being diverse one from another).** The narrative says they were given plenty of the royal wine, which means the finest wine available.

In the wine-making process, wine is poured from vessel to vessel to improve its quality, to separate the liquid from the dregs of the grapes. The implication in the 48th chapter of Jeremiah is that Moab had sat at ease (in one vessel) so long that she had become stale. Moab had not learned the many lessons that would have changed her. These lessons would have come if the country had humbled herself to follow God.

Instead, verse 29 says that Moab was "exceeding proud," lofty, arrogant, and even haughty of heart.

The juice of the grapes is brought into a winery at harvest. Some of the potential wine is placed in particular vessels, that undergo various conditions — heat, cold, dampness, darkness, and so forth. All of those processes are necessary to bring forth the good wine. The winemaker then can draw the wine from each vessel, leaving the sediment in the bottom. After the wine has been placed in vessels turned on their sides, the wine again can be drawn off leaving the sediment on the sides, which are now the "bottoms."

Each step in the process produces a different result. The final result from a good crop (a good "year") of grapes is the "royal wine." The more the process is repeated, the higher the quality of the wine, the more clarity it will have. If the grape juice is not put through this process, it loses its value. It may turn to vinegar, and it certainly has taken on the harsh taste of the sediment itself.

We are like the wine, except that we have wills. We can choose to be poured from one "vessel" — one experience — to another. We can choose to be poured from one change to another, or we can say no to change. We have the right to choose.

Jeremiah said Moab had not gone into captivity. He was not talking about being captured by the enemy, but about the "captivity" of discipline, captivity of "the vessel in place for the process of change."

How many times have you heard people say, "I can't change. That is just part of my personality. I am just like that. I get my temper from my dad or mother. It's hereditary. It is part of my nature."

We might use those excuses back when we had limited horizons, but now our horizons are unlimited. God is wanting to show us the process for change.

A winemaker always will bring forth the correct vessels to refine the wine. He has a specific method, so also does God have a specific method and purpose for our lives. I believe we are in the refinery of the Holy Spirit. God is the master teacher, the master planner, the master refiner, the master developer.

But we have to be willing to allow change in our lives. We have to be willing to be poured from one vessel to another and be separated from the past. There is a purpose to all that is happening in our lives — and we know there is only one purpose for us. That purpose is to be conformed to the image and likeness of Christ. The purpose of all of the refining God does in each of us is to make the flesh so transparent that other people see Jesus in us.

We Have To Choose Change

Romans 8:29 says that those whom He foreknew, He predestinated to be changed into the image of Jesus, the firstborn of many brethren. We must get hold of the vision God has for our lives. We must get hold of the fact that all of the processes of change in our lives, and in the Church, are to accomplish our refining to be more like Christ.

Zechariah 4:6 says that things are not accomplished by man's might nor power but by the Spirit of the Lord. God looks at us as a rich, fragrant, robust, aromatic wine, a royal wine to be poured out from His throne. His design is that you and I go forth as new wine, as the *royal* wine.

We must catch that vision. We must choose what He wants. To know that there will be great works of God is one thing, but to be in a position to be part of those works is another! I do not want to settle for just hearing what others are doing. I want to be part of it. I want to do what God has called me to do.

Have you ever stopped and thought, "Everyone else but me seems to be moving on?"

There is always more pouring and more emptying and more pouring and emptying. To be one of those who is moving on with God, you have to allow the process to take place in your life.

A pastor in California said, "God's activity upon me is the guarantee of the value He places on me and of the ultimate intention He has for me."

You might be going through what seems to be many processes. If so, it shows the value God has placed on you.

Restaurants that have bars attached will have bottles of wine on display. To look at the bottle, you might not know which was expensive and a fine quality and which was a cheap wine. You can buy certain kinds of wine by the gallon that apparently were made from grapes brought into the winery that morning! Perhaps a couple of dollars will buy a gallon.

On the other hand, you can pay thousands of dollars for a "vintage" wine. That is one which has been poured and emptied, poured and emptied, then allowed to age in such a position that the sediment is left in the bottom. Not long ago, a bottle of wine sold in the Napa Valley, California's wine country, for $50,000. The difference in the quality of those two wines is the *process* of refining that went on.

God's activity upon you is the value that He has placed in you and the ultimate intention He has for you. Great ministries are produced from great trials, from being poured from one vessel to another until that process is clarified. I believe there is a direct relationship between great trials and testings and a great anointing. If you want to walk in great power and do the works of God, it will take a great anointing.

Tribulation Worketh Patience

Another thing involved in the production of fine wine is pressure on the grapes. The trials and tribulations of life are the *pressure* on us.

There has been a misunderstanding about trials and tribulations. The Apostle Paul talked about tribulations to the church at Rome.

> **And not only so, but we glory in tribulations also: knowing that tribulation worketh patience.**
>
> **And patience, experience; and experience, hope.**
>
> **Romans 5:3,4**

Tribulations in that verse is the Greek word *thlipsis.* This Greek word is the same word for "afflicted," which means "pressure."[1] You can read that verse as "we glory in pressure, knowing that pressure works patience." And *patience* is the Greek word *hupomone* which means "courageous fortitude."[2]

In the fourth verse, we see that courageous fortitude develops experience, or character. So we see that pressures in life produce courageous fortitude which results in experience, and experience develops hope. Does that sound better than tribulation?

---

[1] *Vine's,* p. 155, Vol. 3; p. 39, Vol. 1.

---

[2] *Strong, James. Strong's Exhaustive Concordance of the Bible* (Hebrew Chaldee Dictionary) (Nashville: Abingdon Press, 1894), p. 14.

Wine connoisseurs talk about the "character" of a certain wine. The pressures that come forth in our Christian walk will produce character, if you stand through them in faith, trusting God for His purpose to be fulfilled. Your stability of character will produce hope — *the hope* of **the mark for the prize of the high calling** (Phil. 3:14).

Another problem with definitions that obscure what the Word is saying in this connection is found in Hebrews 12:7.

> **For whom the Lord loveth he chasteneth, and scourgeth every son whom he receiveth.**
>
> **If ye endure chastening, God dealeth with you as with sons; for what son is he whom the father chasteneth not?**
>
> **But if ye be without chastisement, whereof all are partakers, then are ye bastards, and not sons.**
>
> **Hebrews 12:6-8**

So we can see very well that we have to go through a process of chastisement. Because if we do not, the Bible says we are going to be bastards. So if we are disciples taught of the Lord, there is always going to be chastening. Be obedient to God's will, and great will be your peace and undisturbed composure. I pray this over me and my family every day, particularly our son.

The misunderstanding has come because we have heard people relate *chastening* to a father spanking his son, and that is incorrect. The Greek word *paideuo* there does *not* primarily mean giving a spanking. It means "to train children," suggesting the broad idea of education ...a training gracious and firm."[3]

The chastening of the Lord is for our spiritual rearing and development. *He does not chasten us physically.* He chastens us with His word. So we can see that in our refining, there is both a purpose and a process of God.

The purpose, as I have written, is to cause us to be conformed to the image of Jesus. The process can be the unique arrangements and circumstances of our lives — our personal experiences. One important thing to remember is this: the process is *never ending.* If you think you have made it, you must not still be alive. You must be returned from the beyond! In this life, as long as you are a child of God, His process of refining never ends. None of us has "made it" yet. He is still working on all of us.

God is a loving and caring Father, Who wants to develop character in each of us. He wants to nurture us to maturity. Therefore, there will be a constant dealing with us. Being poured from vessel to vessel will do this. Remember! The value is not on the vessel, but on the wine within that vessel. God does not place value on situations, circumstances, and experiences. He places value on the wine — you. If you reject the "vessel," however, you are rejecting the process of refining. You cannot reject the vessel — the circumstances — and receive the process of development and growth in your life.

[3] *Vine's*, p. 183, Vol. 1.

8
Four Kinds of Vessels

To illustrate the kinds of "vessels" God uses, let us say that a harvest of grapes has been brought in to a very talented winemaker. He knows how to produce the finest, richest, aromatic royal wine. Once the grapes have gone through the process of being squeezed, the fresh juice is placed into a vessel.

Let us say this first vessel is an amber color — but the grape juice is red. When the juice is placed into this vessel, all of a sudden, it has lost its identity. The juice knows it is not amber in color.

"My color is *red*. Hey, out there! Don't you see me? You are looking at me, but I can tell you don't see me. I don't really look this way. I am not really amber. I am not really discolored."

This is called *the vessel of misunderstanding.* Every one of us, at one time or another, has been in a vessel of misunderstanding. People did not understand what we were saying or doing. Our souls suffered pressure because of this.

The winemaker leaves the juice in the amber-colored vessel until the dregs are settled. Then he draws it out of this vessel into another, leaving the harsh-tasting sediment behind. The dregs of this vessel are self-defense, self-vindication, and self-righteousness — all the ways we defend our souls, our "ego."

When you accept the vessel (the process) you will *still* not always be understood. But when you trust God, knowing that this situation will develop character in you, then you will begin to care less about people's opinions. Your only concern will be God's opinion. Going on with God will be your only concern, and the wine that you are has moved a step farther in the refining process.

Then you are placed into another vessel. Let us say this one has a flat bottom. This container does not allow the wine to rise, to bubble up. The vessel feels odd-shaped. It just does not "feel" right. People come and look at it, and you are inside, and you know they are looking at you in this odd shape. This vessel is called *the vessel of public gaze.* This involves public judgments and criticism.

They look at you and say, "Why are you like that? Why did you do that? I would never have done that."

People judge and criticize you, and you do not like it. You want out. However, if you will stop looking at people who are looking at you, but stand still and see what God is doing, you will see that you are losing a portion of yourself that needs to be cut away. You are developing character. The portion you are losing is *pride.* When that situation is fully developed, the winemaker carefully withdraws you.

Now the winemaker puts you in a third vessel, and this one is clay. It is not transparent. You cannot see out of it, and others cannot see into it. Everyone else is outside, and you are inside. You can hear them, and you know what they are doing. You hear the joy and the music, but you are inside the *vessel of isolation.*

And you wonder, "Does anyone know I'm in here?"

This seems a very dark process. This is a damp, cold place. And you do not understand why you are here.

The "wine" wants to say, "Let me out of here. I've had enough!"

In this vessel, sometimes the Lord leaves us all alone. Do you know why? He lets the process work, because in this third process, in the darkness, in the not-understanding, a miracle is coming forth in the wine. The wine is developing that rich aromatic flavor. When the winemaker takes us out of this vessel, what is left behind is *impatience.*

All of the infinite trials of God have a purpose. They all are producing clarity, transparency, and fragrance in our lives.

There is a fourth vessel, and this one is really strange looking. It has some very odd shapes. It is curved here and curved there, like an exotic wine bottle. These bottles are of all different shapes. This one is called *the vessel of strange guidance.*

In this vessel, you are all out of shape. The wine inside the vessel has flowed this way, then that. And you know this bottle is not your shape.

Strange guidance is when you are where God wants you to be, and you can see no rhyme or reason as to why. You have never been there? Just hold on and wait. If you want to move for God, sooner or later, you will be in this vessel.

"God," you will say, "I don't know why You have me here. It makes no sense whatsoever. I see absolutely no purpose in this."

Let me give you an example from my own life:

Once I went to Norway for a scheduled meeting. I had no witness not to go. My "strange" guidance (as it turned out) was to go. After eight hours traveling on the train in areas where snow was up over the buildings, getting on and off to change trains with bags and overseas suitcases, a friend and I stepped off at our destination.

The little train station was closed. No one was there to meet us. We were not in the big cities and towns, but out in the byways. No one spoke English.

Of course, we wondered, "God, have we missed you? This makes no sense whatever. What are we doing here?" But we just waited in faith.

Then the pastor of the church where we had been scheduled to speak arrived. My contact in Oslo had called him after we boarded the train to go to this little town out in the countryside.

We were very happy to see him, as you can imagine, but then he said, "I didn't know you were coming. The meetings were canceled!"

Strange guidance. To try to save the situation, the man had called as many people as he could think of to come for a service.

He said, "I could only get ten people. Will you come and speak to them?"

What else were we going to do? The train station was closed. There was nowhere else to go. So we got in his car and drove another two and a half hours! After all, the Lord says His Word will not return void, so ministry is never wasted. (Is. 55:11.) But where was the rhyme or the reason? How did this happen? It happened because of flesh and a lack of communication.

However, God had His reasons for allowing this. It was "strange guidance" to us, but He knew what He was doing. One of the ten people at the meeting was a woman whose hand was totally paralyzed from three sessions of surgery. All of the nerves were severed, and it was swollen to three times its normal size. Her hand was healed instantly!

Another one of the ten was a woman who could not walk because of multiple sclerosis — and she walked out of the meeting!

In situations that make up the vessel of "strange guidance," you say, "Lord, I don't understand this, but I will go and do what you want me to do."

Although the guidance may seem strange, trust Him and obey. The dregs left behind in this vessel are those of *distrust.*

The Apostle Paul, who had so many great revelations that are the basis of everything we believe today, wrote in his second letter to the Corinthian church about the different "vessels" (processes) he had gone through.

> **Of the Jews five times received I forty stripes save one.**
>
> **Thrice was I beaten with rods, once was I**

> **stoned, thrice I suffered shipwreck, a night and a day I have been in the deep;**
>
> **In journeyings often, in perils of water, in perils of robbers, in perils by mine own countrymen, in perils by the heathen, in perils in the city, in perils in the wilderness, in perils in the sea, in perils among false brethren;**
>
> **In weariness and painfulness, in watchings often, in hunger and thirst, in fastings often, in cold and nakedness.**
>
> **Beside those things that are without, that which cometh upon me daily, the care of all the churches.**
>
> **Who is weak, and I am not weak? who is offended, and I burn not?**
>
> **If I must needs glory, I will glory of the things** (vessels, or processes) **which concern my infirmities** (the dregs in the wine that was Paul).
>
> **2 Corinthians 11:24-30**

Paul was saying, "In spite of all I have gone through, when you suffer, I feel it."

Those processes of situations, circumstances, and experiences developed character in Paul.

Too often, we do not want to go through processes. We think God certainly cannot be in *this!* But do not look at the "vessel" — the container, the experience or circumstance. Look at what is occurring in you through that experience. Look at the end result. Look at the character you are developing.

Each time you are poured from vessel to vessel, you are developed more and more into a rich, fine, aromatic wine.

The Difference Between Purpose and Product

There is a difference between a purpose and a product. The purpose is found in the will of God. The product is found in the life of the believer. God is looking for the product of the fruit of the spirit (Gal. 5:22) to be developed in our lives.

You are going to see fruit come forth in this new wave. You will still see miracles — signs and wonders; however, the lasting fruit of the spirit is what the world out there is going to recognize as being like Jesus.

In Philippians 4:11, Paul told us how to live in the midst of the processes of God:

> **Not that I speak in respect of want: for I have learned, in whatsoever state I am, *therewith to be content.***

Do not worry if you are going through something. Trust God in *every* situation. He can deliver you, and He can bring forth the end result that He desires.

Perhaps there are some things that happen to you that are *not* of God. Then trust Him to find you in it, and deliver you. You can find God in all things that you go through to develop character. (I am not talking about sickness and disease or other things that are of the enemy, not God.) Trust God. He always makes us a way of escape that we might overcome.

Paul learned to be independent of the vessel — the trials and circumstances. He knew *he* had to change, not the situation.

Sometimes human love wants to shelter and protect — but not divine love. That does not mean God is not love, nor that He does not love you. It means He has a greater love than human love. He loves you enough to let you go through things for your good. Delivering you before the process is finished would not be for your good. You would just have to start over in another vessel — or be spoiled wine.

If you give your children everything on a silver platter, they will be spoiled brats. But God gives every good and perfect gift. (James 1:17.) He is the Father of Light. There is no change or variableness in Him. He knows what He wants you to be. He chose you for that before the formation of time. He knows you can be that royal wine. He wants you to be the best.

Isaiah 25:6 gives us another picture.

> **And in this mountain shall the Lord of hosts make unto all people a feast of fat things, a feast of wine on the lees, of fat things full of marrow, of wine on the lees *well refined.***

God glories in what we are becoming: **wine on the lees well refined.** His process works in us to become that ultimate wine. Even at the end, God was saying in this verse from Isaiah, if there are some dregs left, they will be purified out.

Revelation 6:6 says:

> **And I heard a voice in the midst of the four beasts say, A measure of wheat for a penny, and three measures of barley for a penny;** (speaking of famine, drought, dryness — in a spiritual sense,

circumstances) **and see thou hurt not the oil and the wine.**

God is saying to us, "Regardless of situations and circumstances, I have said, **hurt not the oil and the wine."**

We will be a rich, aromatic wine, full-bodied and of a heavenly fragrance — *if* we allow God's process to go forward in our lives to accomplish His purpose in us.

9
Trusting God in Seasons of Change

These are times and seasons of change. What the Church needs to realize is that we have learned to trust God during the good times, but not when things turn dark. We trust God during the sunshine of our lives. We trust Him when things are going right. But when shadows come, and things are not going right, we fall into doubt.

We can trust Him in the springs and summers of our lives, but when the winters come, it becomes difficult to trust. In the springtime, everything is blooming. In the summer, everything is in fruition, and things are great. But what happens when the fall seasons arrive, and winter draws near? We begin to doubt that God is in control. Every believer has all of these seasons occurring in his life.

The "winter" season is a wilderness, a dry spell. No one really wants a winter season; however, those are the seasons that show the internal structure of the character of a person. Those are the climates in which the situations we talked about in the last two chapters occur.

In the summer, there is the foliage, and the internal structure does not show very much. But in the winter, the bare branches and trunks are exposed. You can see what is really there.

In order for us to be developed by God, we must go through the various seasons and the various vessels. When we hit those valleys of transition, we must look to God for our new directions. Today, I believe, we are in a new time frame. We are in a new season with Him.

Psalm 37:40 says, **And the Lord shall help them because they trust in him.** *Because they trust in Him.* Also, you need to know that changes can come even in the summer, in the seasons when things are going right. This happened to me not too long ago.

Within a year and a half, we had a lot of changes in our ministry, and in three years, God opened nineteen different nations and countries to us. Change is not always bad, as I have said before. It does not have to be painful, if you will trust in Him.

We began as an evangelistic ministry, holding miracle healing crusades. Then God added open doors to minister in churches, and began taking us overseas. And one day in June of 1986, I was in California praying about a meeting set for that evening, and the Holy Spirit interrupted me. Have you ever had that happen?

First He drew my attention to the east coast of the United States, then He said to me concerning 1988, 1989, and 1990, "Valerie, there is a change coming."

To be honest, my first reaction was, "Get thee behind me, Satan!"

Why would God be speaking change to me? Doors of utterance were opening. Invitations for overseas were coming in; finances were coming in. The anointing was operating, and the Word of God was going forth. Were all these things not a sign that we were in the flow of what God was doing? Were they not a sign that we were in His perfect will? That was my reaction.

I thought, "If things were not working, if doors were not opening, if finances dried up, then it would be a sign of change. I would begin to ask God where I had missed Him."

But we do not usually stop and ask God when things are going right. Yet, we should — especially during these critical times in the Spirit.

The Holy Spirit said, "Valerie, I want you to minister more on the East Coast."

That really did not thrill me. I loved people on the East Coast, but I did not want to spend more time there. Then when He added that He wanted me to spend more time specifically in New England, that thrilled me less. I did not want to "go back to Nazareth." New England is my Nazareth. But I found that you do things God's way, even when you might not think there is a need for change. If He is speaking, it is time for change. It is time!

Do not try to figure out God. That will not work. You may be going through a time and season of change, but God is not. He never changes His basic character, principles, and ways. His plan for the earth has not changed: to have a people who will love, worship, and obey Him by choice. However, do not expect Him to meet you the same way, because He *does* use various methods to achieve His unchanging purposes.

We are in a critical period of time. The next few years are a time of preparation for what God is going to do after 1990. If Jesus has not returned by that time, we will see the beginnings of a move of God greater than any we have ever experienced. This is a time of preparation, a time of positioning.

To get positioned, we need to be on the right path, the path God has set before us.

The Path of the Just

I am convinced from reading Scripture and from taking time with the Father that there is a pathway for each and every believer. I believe that before the formation of time, Almighty God ordained a particular pathway. There are six scriptures that I want to look at in this context.

> 1. **Trust in the Lord with all thine heart and lean not unto thine own understanding.**
>
> 2. **In all they ways acknowledge him, and he shall direct thy paths.**
>
> **Proverbs 3:5,6**
>
> 3. **But the path of the just** (or righteous) **is as the shining light that shineth more and more unto *the* perfect day.**
>
> **Proverbs 4:18**
>
> 4. **There is a path which no fowl knoweth, and which the vulture's eye hath not seen: The lion's whelps have not trodden it, nor the fierce lion passed by it.**
>
> **Job 28:7,8** (Treated as one verse.)

5. **Now the just** (or righteous) **shall live by faith: but if any man draw back, my soul shall have no pleasure in him.**

Hebrews 10:38

6. **For my thoughts are not your thoughts, neither are my ways your ways, saith the Lord.**

Isaiah 55:8

The path of the just is a shining light, according to Proverbs 4:18, that brightens more and more as it runs on toward the perfect day. Notice that the Holy Spirit said *the* perfect day, not a perfect day, in that verse. *The perfect day* is talking about the coming of the Lord Jesus Christ. It is talking about the day when He comes.

In Matthew 24:36, Jesus said that *no man* knows the exact day or hour of His second coming. But to believers, He will not come as a thief in the night (Rev. 16:15) — if they keep their *garments* (of righteousness) on. Only to unbelievers will His coming be a total and horrifying surprise like a thief who breaks into your house in the middle of the night.

We may not know the exact hour or the exact day, but I believe that within the spirit of the believer who walks the path of the just, there will be a "knowing" as *the* day draws nearer. The glory will become brighter and brighter, then all of a sudden, it will be very close!

God has that pathway for every believer; not just for the leaders or those in the fivefold offices, but for every single believer. Walking that path is like walking upward toward the sun — if we could. The closer you got, the brighter it would become. And the closer we get to the Son of God, the brighter the path gets.

Similarities Between Eagles and Vultures

When I began to study God's pathways several years ago, I found the verse in Job about a path that even the vultures have not seen. Then once I was studying a lot about eagles, because as Christians, we refer to ourselves as "eagles." And I found there is a close similarity between eagles and vultures. Not in all respects, of course, but in some.

Both have the ability to soar to great heights; both have extremely far-seeing vision.

One example I like to use comes from old cowboy movies or films about the French Foreign Legion. In many of them, there will be a scene where you see a guy walking across a desert. His clothes are ragged; he is dirty and sweaty; and his footsteps are dragging. He is looking for water.

Then in the next scene, you always see the vultures circling around above him. I found that a vulture has an instinct to know when a person — or animal — is on his last legs. Whether they determine this by the slower movements or what, I do not know. But somehow, they know when to close in.

In the films, you see this vulture looking down on this staggering man and almost pinpointing where he will fall. They would be waiting when he was totally exhausted, collapsed, and could not move another step.

But the Word of God says there is a path vultures cannot see! I believe it is the path of the just, referred to in Proverbs 4:18. I believe we are on that pathway, the one Almighty God set for us before He created the world. When we are pressing on toward the mark where the prize of the high calling will be accomplished, we are on a path upward.

If we are truly on that path, the "fowls" (demons) will not be able to see us and attack as they have in times past. Yes, we endure an onslaught of warfare. But God is not a defeated God. He is a victorious God. And I believe there is a path the fowls will not know. As keen as the eyesight of the fowls is, as high as they can soar, they will not see where we are in God.

God says on this path, it is not only vultures that will not see, but the lion's whelps. It is not the old lion in the jungle that we fear attacks from — it is the young lions. The young lion moves out quietly and begins to track its prey. The young lion is the one that captures the victim and brings it back to the old lion, lying in wait.

God said even the lion's whelps will not trod on that path, and the fierce lion will pass it by.

Stay in the Middle of the Flow

In 1987, I was flying from Atlanta back to Florence, South Carolina, by way of Myrtle Beach. I had just finished reading a book, when I happened to look out the window. It was no big spiritual thing. No light came upon me.

There was no booming voice saying, "Valerie, look out of the window."

I just looked out of the plane, and I saw a river. This was different than a lot of other rivers I have seen. This was a real winding river, and in all of its curves and turns, you could see tributaries flowing into it. Some tributaries were big, others were small, but down the whole length of the river that I could see were these side avenues.

Then the Holy Spirit spoke and said, "Valerie, that is typical of the Body of Christ. If you would stay in the middle of the flow of the river, even though it is going to turn and wind, you will always end up at the right spot. But if you stay too far over to the right, or too far over to the left, it is going to be too much of a temptation to go down these "rabbit trails" of streams. That may not be too bad, but you will not end up accomplishing what I want you to accomplish."

He said, "I have never said the pathway would be straight. It will have turns, but if it turns and you are in the middle of the flow, you will end up where you are supposed to be."

So during 1988 and thus far in 1989, there have been changes in the lives of many believers and changes in the Church as a whole. Different seasons have come and will be coming in the realm of the Spirit. Do not lock God in to one pattern, because He will not allow you to limit Him. Do not be devastated when things change: simply change with the flow of God. Stay in the center of His will and His timing.

Every single one of us has a place in His plan. I cannot fulfill your goal, and you cannot fulfill mine. God wants us to make it exactly to His perfect will —

not one measure, one ounce less. God has confidence in you, because He has confidence in Himself that He is capable of bringing you to the goal — if you will allow Him to do so.

During the times of change in my life and ministry, I have learned some things. I learned to trust God in all seasons, not just in the summer when the sun shines, not just when things are going well.

I have learned to trust Him in those times when transitions occur, and I want to cry out, "God, where are You? Did You go out to lunch?"

Perhaps you dial Jeremiah 33:3 — **Call unto me, and I will answer...**— and get a busy signal. Perhaps you come boldly to the throne, and it has an "out to lunch" sign on it. I am sure you understand what I am saying. I have felt that way in times past, when I found myself going through different things.

As I said before, I have found that change is nothing more than the earthly name for the School of the Holy Spirit.

The main thing in trusting God is to know that you know that you know that He is the *one in control* — not you.

I have discovered that five things change during times of transition, and I want you to be able to recognize when these things are changing. That will help you stay in the middle of God's river-path for you. Understanding these things will help you trust God.

10
Five Things of God That Change

The five things of God that change during times of transition are: Resources, methods, weapons, images (or ways we see ourselves), and ways of thinking.

First, look at Elijah the Tishbite, beginning in First Kings 17. Before that chapter in the Bible, there is no mention of Elijah. We do not even know what a Tishbite is — a people or a place! But suddenly, there Elijah is: a full-blown prophet of God.

> **And Elijah the Tishbite, who was of the inhabitants of Gilead, said unto Ahab, As the Lord God of Israel liveth, before whom I stand, there shall not be dew nor rain these years, but according to my word.**
>
> **1 Kings 17:1**

Compare this to someone just coming out of Bible school, or even someone who has been in the ministry for a while. Suppose it is your graduation day, and suddenly the Lord says:

"I want you to go to the governor of the State of New Jersey and tell him it is not going to rain for three years."

Basically, that is what happened to Elijah. Not knowing anything about Elijah before this, we can relate it to someone all of a sudden getting a word from the Lord. So Elijah got the direction of the Lord, and he went to King Ahab and told him what God had said.

> **And the Word of the Lord came unto him, saying,**
>
> **Get thee hence, and turn thee eastward, and hide thyself by the brook Cherith, that is before Jordan.**
>
> **1 Kings 17:2,3**

That was a short-lived ministry! He had a ministry to kings, when all of a sudden, the Word of the Lord came saying, "Go a different direction."

This time, the Lord wanted Elijah to go eastward.

Perhaps, the prophet was thinking, "You want me to go east? This is going to be exciting. I was pretty good with kings. I can hardly wait for *this* assignment."

So he goes east, and as he walks, the Lord speaks again and says, "You will find a brook by the name of Cherith, and when you get there, I want you to hide."

"Boy," Elijah may have thought, "this assignment must be great. The other one was to a king. Now, I can just imagine the ambush I'm going to be involved in. I can hardly wait. I am sure God is going to have me doing some tremendous thing, and it will be publicized."

But the Lord said, "Elijah, when you are hiding behind that brook, I want you to drink from it."

"You want me to drink from it? All right. I guess I am kind of thirsty. I could stand a drink."

Then the Lord said, "By the way, while you are drinking from it, I am going to have the ravens come and feed you."

"Why would the ravens feed me, Lord?"

"Because, Elijah, you are going to be there for a while. In fact, you are going to be there three and a half years, and the ravens are going to bring you bread and meat."

That would not excite me too much, because I know what ravens eat. They eat garbage and trash. I would not have been too thrilled, and I do not expect Elijah was either. However, what I want you to see is that in times of change, your resources are changed.

Number One: Resources Change

God provided for Elijah when he went to the king, but then He sent the prophet to the brook, and his resource was to be dirty birds.

Then we see in verse seven that the brook dried up.

"God, I thought you were going to provide for me. You told me to hide by this brook. You told me to drink the water and be fed by ravens, now the brook has dried up."

Resources change — but the Provider does not change.

From there, the Word of the Lord came again: "I want you to go to Zarephath, Elijah."

In the natural, it looks as if the prophet has moved down a few pegs. First he went to kings, then he was fed by birds and lived in safety by a brook;

now, he is to have still another resource — a widow woman who is not even of the people of Israel.

When the Word of the Lord comes, your earthly resource may change. Many times in seasons of change, we expect God to meet us in the same way He always has. He is not going to do that. He will always provide, but not always by the same means, the same earthly resource.

Elijah went to Zarephath, and you know the story of how he was fed supernaturally. The widow and her son also were fed, because they obeyed the Word of the Lord through the prophet. Later, the son was even raised from the dead. People who obey God and help you during times of transition will be blessed as well as you.

In First Kings 18, the Lord sent Elijah back to the king. His ministry direction was changed once again. Once there, Elijah had Ahab call in all of the four hundred and fifty prophets of Baal and the four hundred prophets of the grove. He arranged a trial, a confrontation on top of Mount Carmel.

First the pagan prophets built their altar and tried for hours every way they knew to get their gods to answer — but there was no response. Then Elijah rebuilt the altar of the Lord that had been broken down. *First of all, he brought restoration.*

Then he took twelve stones — denoting authority — and made a sacrifice, which was consumed along with the stones and the water around the altar. Then he slaughtered the prophets. After that, he prayed seven times for rain, and the rains came for the first time in three and a half years.

Elijah was so anointed, he outran the chariots of the king back to town. (1 Kings 18:46.)

In First Kings 19:1-8, we see the next change of resource. A messenger came to Elijah from the queen, Jezebel. She had just learned that her priests had been killed. Her messengers came to Elijah's house and knocked on the door.

They said, "Is there anyone home?"

Elijah answered, "I am here."

"Would you sign for this? It's a special delivery for you."

"Oh, sure." He signed and ripped it open, then began to tremble.

"Hurry up, servant. We have to get out of here. This is from Jezebel. She says that if her gods do not do to me this day what I did to her prophets that she will do it herself. Hurry up! Let's go."

He and his servant went to Beersheba, and he left the servant there and went on to the wilderness where he found a juniper tree. The Word of the Lord had not come unto Elijah to run into the wilderness, yet God provided for him anyway. Under the juniper tree, we see yet another new resource for Elijah — an angel.

As Elijah slept, an angel baked him a cake of bread and brought a pitcher of water. What does that say to us? When your heart is right before God, even if you miss His direction, He still will provide. Elijah's heart was right, but he was moved by the flesh. Fear overcame him so that he ran away from trouble.

He ate the angel's bread and drank the water, and survived on the strength of it forty days.

Supernaturally, if necessary, God will provide, but the resources He uses for you change in seasons of change.

Number Two: Methods Change

The best scriptural example I could find for the changing of methods is in Luke 5:1-11 where the multitude pressed in on Jesus as He taught them.

He was on the shore of the Lake of Gennesaret when the crowds pressed on him. He turned around and saw two empty boats. The fishermen were on shore washing their nets. Jesus asked whose boats they were, and Peter responded that they were his.

Jesus then got into one of the boats in order to have room to teach without being overwhelmed. After he was through, he turned to Peter.

Jesus said, "Peter, have you caught any fish?"

Peter said no, and Jesus said, "Change the direction of your boat. Launch out into the deep part of the lake here."

This was a change in method for the fishermen.

Peter could have said, "Lord, you don't understand. I am familiar with these waters. This is my trade, my profession. I have been a fisherman all my life. You are telling me to go out into the deep. Obviously, you don't know anything about fishing or you wouldn't say that. In net fishing, you don't go out deep. You fish in the shallows.

"Also, you told me to cast over the right side, when anyone knows that if you are a net fisherman, you cast over the left and drag the net."

But methods change. Jesus said it, and Peter obeyed. The result was such a large catch that the net broke. Then they brought over the second boat, and both were filled so full of fish that they began to sink. After that, Peter, James, and John left the trade of fishing and followed Jesus fishing for men.

Another person who had to deal with changed methods was Naaman in the Old Testament. The story is found in Second Kings 5. Naaman was captain of the host of the king of Syria, and on one of their raids, a little Israelite girl had been captured. She was now a servant in the house of Naaman, who was a leper.

One day, this servant said to Naaman's wife, "If he would go to Israel, there is a prophet who could heal your husband."

Naaman, a respected man for his bravery in war, went to the king of Syria and asked for a letter of introduction to the king of Israel. When the king of Israel opened the letter and found out that the captain of all of Syria's armies with an entire entourage was on his doorstep wanting to be healed, he panicked and went into outrage.

The Israelite king rent his clothes, in those days a sign of great distress, and said, "Am I God that I can cause one to live and another to die?"

Elisha heard about it and sent for Naaman to come see him. However, when the great man arrived,

Elisha did not even come out and talk to him. He sent his servant to tell Naaman to bathe in the Jordan River seven times, and he would be healed.

That offended Naaman greatly! He was accustomed to seeing people bow before him, and probably he expected sacrifices to be made and offerings to some god. At any rate, Elisha's *method* of achieving his healing was new and unexpected, also distasteful. There were cleaner, prettier rivers in Syria.

There is a new anointing today coming from the throne of God. This is a purer anointing than we have ever experienced. The anointing that worked miracles in times past is not going to be good enough for today. It was perfect for those moves of God, but it will not be for the new move of the Holy Spirit. We must not try to lock God in to ministering to us in the same way He did previously.

At any rate, Naaman eventually was talked into trying what Elisha said, and he bathed seven times and was healed. Seven is God's number of perfection, God's number of completion. His methods of achieving things in our lives may change, but His perfection never changes.

Number Three: Weapons Change

In First Samuel 17, we see David as a young boy at the battle with the Philistines whose champion was Goliath. David was surprised that no one was dealing with this man who dared to defy the armies of the living God.

When he was brought before King Saul and

offered to kill the giant, Saul said, "You're just a youth. How can you go up against this giant?"

David replied by telling Saul of killing a lion and a bear, and Saul got excited. Apparently, however, he missed the part about the Lord *delivering* David from the lion and the bear. He began to try to outfit David with full armor up to the helmet and to arm him with his own large sword.

David came out of the dressing room hardly able to walk because everything was too big and weighed him down.

With God, *weapons change in warfare.*

David said, "O King, I cannot move with these on. I'm not a soldier, and I have not tried these things out to see if I can handle them."

Saul said, "What are you going to use then?"

So David pulled out his sling shot. Can you imagine standing with a sling shot before the king of Israel, who is a mighty warrior, the head of a big, strong army?

The Word says that as David crossed the brook between the armies, he caught up five smooth stones. Zechariah 12:10 and Hebrews 10:29 says that the Holy Spirit is the Spirit of grace. Five is the number of grace and the number of the Holy Spirit. David only used one stone, but he picked up five. He picked up the Spirit of grace to give him direction. He walked in the wisdom of the Spirit of God.

He took those five stones, and let one fly at Goliath. That one hit the giant in the forehead, and he fell on his face. However, David did not stop there.

He went and used Goliath's own sword to cut off his head. The giant's sword probably was even bigger than Saul's, but David knew when it was time to change weapons.

Sometimes we get comfortable with our weapons of warfare. The Word says they are not carnal but mighty. They are mighty before God for a purpose — the pulling down of strongholds. (2 Cor. 10:4.) However, the weapons we have used in the past may not be the weapons necessary for today. The Word of God does say that at the name of Jesus every knee shall bow (Phil. 2:10). But under that overall canopy of authority, the weapons may change.

I am very aggressive in prayer. Sometimes I get loud only because it builds faith to hear someone pray — even myself. Also, God is not deaf, and the devil's not deaf, but sometimes I am so mad at the devil that I get loud.

Once, my son heard me praying loudly, and he came down stairs in all innocence and said, "What did the devil do this time?"

But suppose that was the only weapon of warfare that I wanted to use, and suppose God spoke and said, "Valerie, will you shut up?"

"But, God, it works. God, I have used this weapon against the devil. I have pulled down that stronghold every single time."

"That's fine, Valerie, but weapons change."

"You mean you want me to be quiet? You want me to praise You?"

Weapons change; however, their power remains the same. God the Provider never changes. His power never changes. Resources change, methods change, weapons change, but not God.

Number Four: Images Change

In seasons of change, there are times we need to change our images. Any of these changes merits a fuller study, but I am simply touching on each one in this book. For an example of necessary image changes and the results, look at the book of Esther.

Esther was an orphan girl of the tribe of Benjamin who had been carried away during the time when the first group of the Nation of Judah was taken into captivity by Nebuchadnezzar. Esther and her cousin Mordecai, however, were now in the court of the king of Persia. Her parents were dead, and she had been brought up by Mordecai, who had the position of sitting in the king's gate. He had taught Esther in the ways of the God of Judah.

When Queen Vashti refused to be put on display before the king's guests at a special royal banquet, King Ahasuerus divorced her. Then he had all the fair young virgins of his one hundred and twenty-seven provinces brought to the palace that he might choose another wife. Mordecai brought Esther into the palace as a candidate for queen.

Esther was a well-brought-up young lady, accustomed to submitting to the Lord and proper authorities. Therefore, she found favor with the keeper of the women in the king's house. He saw that she had everything she needed during the year of preparation to go before the king. The chamberlain gave Esther and her seven ladies in waiting the best place in the house of the women.

During the year, the women were to use oil of myrrh six months and sweet odors and other things for the other six months. Probably they were taught manners, fashions, perhaps a musical instrument, or whatever the king particularly liked. They were taught to present an entirely different image when they went to the king than the one they presented on entering the preparation chambers.

After a year, each girl was to go and present herself to the king for one night. In the morning, she would go into a second house of women, where the concubines lived. After that, she had all her needs met, but she would not see the king unless she had found such favor with him that he asked for her by name.

We of the Church have settled for the House of Concubines. We settle for getting all of our needs met, instead of seeking the King. We seek everything God can give us instead of seeking first the Kingdom of God. There are many who are in the House of Concubines. They will make it to heaven some day, but I do not believe they will come into the full presence of the King. There are certain preparations necessary to find the King's favor and be ready to meet Him face to face.

These girls could have anything they asked for, but the Word says Esther **required nothing but what Hegai the king's chamberlain, the keeper of the women, appointed** (Esth. 2:15). She was obedient to authority. And she found favor with everyone who looked at her, the Bible says.

When she had her turn, he loved her above all the other women. She found grace and favor in the king's sight more than all of the others. He made her queen instead of Vashti.

If Esther had not gone through an image change — from a little Benjamite girl from the land of Judah to a queen — her people in the entire land of the Medes and Persians would have been massacred. A plot was put forth against the Jews because Mordecai refused to bow down to Haman, whom the king recently had elevated to royal status.

Mordecai told Esther she must intervene with the king, which was illegal and could have resulted in her head being cut off. She sent word that she had not been called to the king's presence for the past thirty days.

Then Mordecai wrote her a note saying, "You will not escape even in the king's house. If you do not help us, God will send help from some other source, but you and your father's house will be destroyed. Who knows but what you were born into this kingdom for such a time as this?" (Esth. 4:14.)

So she went through another process of change, fasted for three days and nights along with all of the rest of her people, and took her life in her hands to approach the king. She had favor with the king, and he extended the scepter to her allowing her to speak to him.

There was a happy ending — at least for the Jews:

Haman and his ten sons were hanged, along with five hundred men in the capital city who had been involved with the plot, and another three hundred the next day. In the other provinces, the Jews slew seventy-five thousand people. Mordecai was promoted second to the king. And the Jewish people in the one hundred and twenty-seven provinces of the Medes and Persians lived in peace. The two days when the Jews turned the tables and killed their enemies are kept, by order of Queen Esther, as the holiday of Purim even until today.

In a time of warfare for her people, Esther changed her image twice — from a young, sheltered Jewish girl to a princess and concubine, and then through her daring and diplomacy in the crisis, she apparently grew to be a mature and adroit queen loved by all. Some books say that one of her descendants was Cyrus, the king of Persia who conquered Babylon some seventy years later and allowed the Jews there to return to the Promised Land. If so, then her change of image had far-reaching consequences.

Number Five: Ways of Thinking Change

The fifth thing that has to change is our way of thinking. In Romans 12, Paul wrote:

> **I beseech you therefore, brethren, by the mercies of God, that ye present your bodies a living sacrifice, holy, acceptable unto God, which is your reasonable service.**

And be not conformed to this world: but be ye transformed by the renewing of your mind. That ye may prove what is that good, and acceptable, and perfect, will of God.

Romans 12:1,2

Your mind must be renewed to the will of God. Proverbs 4:20-22 says:

My son, attend to my words; incline thine ear unto my sayings.

Let them not depart from thy eyes; keep them in the midst of thy heart.

Why? Because **they are life unto those that find them, and health to all their flesh.**

Second Corinthians 3:18 says:

But we all, with open face beholding as in a glass the glory of the Lord, are changed into the same image from glory to glory, even as by the Spirit of the Lord.

As you allow the Word of God to be a mirror reflecting your life, you will be changed from glory to glory into the image of Jesus. Your mind will be renewed to the very perfect will of God.

What happens in the perfect will of God? You will seek Him with your whole heart. Thank God that He is our healer and our provider, but I will seek after Him — not after what He can do for me, but for His own sake.

Look at Romans 12:1,2 in *The Amplified Bible:*

I appeal to you therefore, brethren, and beg of you in view of [all] the mercies of God, to make a decisive dedication of your bodies — presenting all your members and faculties — as a living sacrifice, holy (devoted, consecrated) and well

pleasing to God, which is your reasonable (rational, intelligent) service and spiritual worship.

Do not be conformed to this world — this age, fashioned after and adapted to its external, superficial customs. But be transformed (changed) by the [entire] renewal of your mind — by its new ideals and its new attitude — so that you may prove [for yourselves] what is the good and acceptable and perfect will of God, even the thing which is good and acceptable and perfect [in His sight for you].

Your thinking has to change. God says His ways are higher than yours or mine. And His thoughts are higher than ours. (Is. 55:9.)

There is no point in saying, "God, how are you going to do this? God, how is this move going to be?"

He does not have to tell us another thing if He does not want to. Stop trying to figure out what God is going to do. Stop trying to figure out the plans and purposes of God. When He has revealed something to you, do what your hands find to do.

Summary of Things That Change

Resources change, but not the Provider.

Methods change, so do not get locked into tradition. Do not get locked into assumptions that God is going to move the same way every time. If He wants you to lay on hands, He will tell you to do that. If He wants to accomplish His purpose another way, do not *assume* you are to lay on hands. Wait for the witness, then obey.

Weapons change. You will not always be led to pray the same way, or to operate in deliverance the same way.

Images change. If you have the wrong image of yourself, if the way you look at yourself is based on the past or on wrong information about yourself, it is time to get the image God has of you. It is time during this season of change to really *see* who you are in Christ. Allow the Holy Spirit to take you to the "house of preparation" for the brides, the place in the spirit where you can be transformed into royalty.

Thinking changes. Renew your mind with the Word so that it will never operate contrary to the Lord's again. How do you know if it is God speaking to you? What you hear will witness in your spirit and will line up with the Word. He speaks in *spirit and in truth.* It will have both, if it is God.

For more information about this ministry, or for additional copies of this book, please write to:

Valerie S. DePastino Ministries, Inc.
P. O. Box 31
Southington, CT 06489

About the Author

Dr. Valerie S. DePastino is an anointed minister whose teaching and preaching ministry is received internationally.

She is the author of two previous books, *Identification of Intercession (A Manual of Intercession)* and *Endtime Commissions Endtime Anointings Ezra 8:36*.

A former public school teacher, Dr. DePastino has earned degrees in psychology, education, and theology. An ordained minister, she is affiliated with several major ministerial fellowships.

Her ministry is characterized by an overwhelming manifestation of the *agape* love of God and is punctuated by powerful manifestations of the gifts of the Holy Spirit as many people receive healings, miracles, and deliverance from all manner of oppression. She also is widely recognized for the manifestation of the Holy Spirit's gift of prophecy to the Body which operates through her.

Dr. DePastino serves as a board member of the Encouragers, a ministry to women in Christian leadership, and as a field representative for Faith Christian Fellowship International Church, Inc.

She resides with her husband, John, and their son, Clarke, in Southington, Connecticut.

David
01634 404349
07752 803515